PREPARING
FOR YOUR
MISSION

PREPARING
FOR YOUR
MISSION

ED J. AND PATRICIA PINEGAR

Deseret Book Company
Salt Lake City, Utah

ISBN 0-87579-646-X

Printed in the United States of America
10   9   8   7   6   5   4   3   2   1

CONTENTS

SECTION 4

THE WORK

ACKNOWLEDGMENTS

Our deepest gratitude goes to the wonderful missionaries we have served with, who, by their great work, have brought many souls to Christ by the power of the Spirit.

Thanks to Dr. Don Norton, who helped in editing, and to the wonderful people at Deseret Book who were so positive with their response and input—Ron Millett, Eleanor Knowles, and Sheri Dew. We'd also like to thank the production team at Deseret Book for their fine work on *Preparing for Your Mission:* Richard Tice, Tonya Facemyer, Patricia Parkinson, Craig Geertsen, Richard Erickson, Linda Nimori, Carole Cole, Rebecca Chambers, Stephanie Bird, Bronwyn Boyd, and Anne Sheffield.

INTRODUCTION

The purpose of missionary work is to bring souls to Christ. As a missionary, you are to prepare yourself to become an instrument in the hands of the Lord in acting as his ambassador—even the Savior's representative.

To prepare to do this requires effort. This workbook can help you (1) gain the vision of Heavenly Father's work, (2) realize the changes you need to make in order to become Christlike and personally worthy to do the work, (3) recognize the things you need to do in order to gain the knowledge, skills, and talents to bring souls to Christ, (4) understand the work in the mission field in finding, teaching, and baptizing Heavenly Father's children, and (5) come to know the joy of serving your Father in Heaven, your Savior, and your fellowman in building up the kingdom of God.

Like all things that are good, completing this workbook requires faith, diligence, patience, perseverance, and commitment. As you proceed through the workbook, you will begin to become the kind of missionary that the Lord wants you to be. Remember, you will be blessed as you prepare to serve the Lord with all your heart, might, mind, and strength.

We testify to you of the truthfulness of the four great points of emphasis in missionary work: first, the sacredness of saving souls and the importance of greatly increasing the number of convert baptisms; second, the need to increase personal faith in order that convert baptisms will increase significantly and dramatically; third, the importance of missionaries prayerfully setting personal convert baptismal goals; fourth, the urgency of being actively and productively engaged in member-missionary work in order that the Lord's harvest may be accomplished. (See Ezra Taft Benson, "President Kimball's Vision of Missionary Work," *Ensign,* July 1985, p. 11.)

This workbook is designed to assist you. The real key, however, to your knowledge and your growth in the Spirit is the scriptures, the word of God. For this reason, the workbook is based on the Standard Works and on the teachings of modern-day prophets.

As you prepare, you will be introduced to additional helps prepared by the Church: the *Missionary Guide,* the *Missionary Gospel Study Guide,* and the discussions. Missionary tapes and videos are also available from Church distribution and LDS bookstores. Visits with former missionaries and mission presidents can assist as well. Religion 130 offered at LDS institutes and Church schools is a terrific course for prospective missionaries. Your stake may also offer a missionary preparation course.

Remember to do your part in preparation. The Lord is always ready to do his. As you prepare, you will not fear, and the Lord will give you the strength you need to succeed.

CHAPTER 1

THE VISION

Heavenly Father's plan is to achieve the salvation of his children. Everything he has given us is to help us gain eternal life. Two of the most important means he has set up to realize this plan are the gospel of Jesus Christ and the restored church. Our duty is to assist our Heavenly Father and our Savior in proclaiming the gospel, perfecting the Saints, and redeeming the dead—thus inviting all to come unto Christ and be perfected in him.

1. What is your Heavenly Father's purpose—his work and his glory? Moses 1:39.

2. Why did the Lord suffer for all and sacrifice his life? What will bring you great joy? Doctrine and Covenants 18:10–16.

3. How did your Heavenly Father show his love for you? John 3:16.

4. How did Christ show his love for you? 2 Nephi 26:24.

5. What was the great charge Christ gave to his disciples? Mark 16:15.

6. What did the Lord tell the Whitmer brothers would be of most worth to them? Doctrine and Covenants 15:6; 16:6.

7. It's important that everyone has a chance to hear the gospel. What do you notice in these revelations given in the Doctrine and Covenants concerning where to preach the word?

   a. 49:1.

   b. 52:22–23, 25–27.

   c. 60:6–8.

   d. 80:1–3.

   e. 106:1–2.

   f. 108:6.

   g. 122:28.

8. Who does the Lord want to be converted and baptized so they may have life everlasting? In 2 Nephi 26:33, Nephi describes who the Lord invites to partake of his goodness. List these kinds of people.

9. In the Book of Mormon, the sons of Mosiah had the vision of missionary work. List the places they taught the Lamanites. Alma 26:29.

Answering the questions and doing the activities in this chapter will help you understand how much your Heavenly Father loves his children. His entire work and glory is in the blessing and perfecting of all men and women. He has set up the plan of salvation to accomplish these things. Surely souls are precious to your Heavenly Father, and your duty in his eternal plan is to assist in the great work of bringing souls to Christ so they might return to the presence of your Father in Heaven.

The Lord hopes that his missionaries will start to feel as the sons of Mosiah felt concerning the welfare of their brothers and sisters here upon the earth: "Now they were desirous that salvation should be declared to every creature, for they could not bear that any human soul should perish; yea, even the very thoughts that any soul should endure endless torment did cause them to quake and tremble." (Mosiah 28:3.)

The feeling of concern for your fellowman is a reflection of your love of God and the pure love of Christ that is within you. When you feel this love, you will have a desire to preach and teach the word of God to all mankind so that they might have everlasting life. As you prepare to serve, you will begin to increase your capacity to love—step by step—and catch the vision of the Lord's work.

THINGS TO DO

1. Visit a Primary Class. While looking at the the children, imagine life without the gospel.

2. Study the world map and envision the number of missionaries needed to take the gospel to the entire world.

3. Read the following statements by the prophets. Then underline or highlight important points.

Joseph Smith: After all that has been said, the greatest and most important duty is to preach the Gospel.

—*History of The Church of Jesus Christ of Latter-day Saints,* 2nd ed. (Salt Lake City: Deseret Book Company, 1980), 2:478.

Joseph Smith: The standard of truth has been erected: no unhallowed hand can stop the work from progressing, persecution may rage, mobs may combine, armies may assemble, calumny may defame, but the truth of God will go forth boldly, nobly, and independent till it has penetrated every continent, visited every clime, swept every country, and sounded in every ear, till the purposes of God shall be accomplished and the great Jehovah shall say the work is done.

—"Church History," *Times and Seasons,* 1 March 1842, p. 709.

Ezra Taft Benson: As Latter-day Saints everywhere, with personal testimonies of these great events, we accept humbly, gratefully, this major responsibility placed upon the Church. We are happy to be engaged in a partnership with our Heavenly Father in the great work of the salvation and exaltation of his children. Willingly we give of our time and our means with which he may bless us to the establishment of his kingdom in the earth. This we know is our first duty and our great opportunity. This spirit has characterized the missionary work of the church of Jesus Christ in all ages. It has been an outstanding mark of the ushering in of the dispensation of the fulness of times—our time. Wherever faithful Latter-day Saints are to be found, this spirit of unselfish sacrifice for the greatest cause in all the earth exists. In a statement published to the world during the last world war, the First Presidency of the Church declared: "No act of ours or of the Church must interfere with this God-given mandate." (Conference Report, April 1942, p. 91.)

—Conference Report, April 1974, p. 155.

Boyd K. Packer: Since baptism is essential there must be an urgent concern to carry the message of the gospel of Jesus Christ to every nation, kindred, tongue, and people. That came as a commandment from Him.

His true servants will be out to convert all who will hear to the principles of the gospel and they will offer them that one baptism which He proclaimed as essential. . . . The powerful missionary spirit and the vigorous missionary activity in The Church of Jesus Christ of Latter-day Saints becomes a very significant witness that the true gospel and that the authority are possessed here in the Church. We accept the responsibility to preach the gospel to every person on earth. And if the question is asked, "You mean you are out to convert the entire world?" the answer is, "Yes. We will try to reach every living soul."

Some who measure that challenge quickly say, "Why, that's impossible! It cannot be done!"

To that we simply say, "Perhaps, but we shall do it anyway."

—Conference Report, October 1975, p. 145.

Spencer W. Kimball: When we have increased the missionaries from the organized areas of the Church to a number close to their potential, that is, every able and worthy boy in the Church on a mission; when every stake and mission abroad is furnishing enough missionaries for that country; when we have used our qualified men to help the apostles to open these new fields of labor; when we have used the satellite and related discoveries to their greatest potential and all of the media—the papers, magazines, television, radio—all in their greatest power; when we have organized numerous other stakes which will be springboards; when we have recovered from inactivity the numerous young men who are now unordained and unmissioned and unmarried; then, and not until then, shall we approach the insistence of our Lord and Master to go into all the world and preach the gospel to every creature.

—*The Teachings of Spencer W. Kimball,* edited Edward L. Kimball (Salt Lake City: Bookcraft, 1982), p. 585.

CHAPTER 2

YOUR DIVINE ROLE AND RESPONSIBILITY

Your duty, opportunity, and blessing are to be an instrument in the hands of the Lord to take the gospel to every nation, kindred, tongue, and people. This is the duty of members as well as full-time missionaries.

1. You were a special individual in your premortal earth life. According to Alma 13:3–7, men are called to the priesthood to do the wonderful work of God here upon the earth. Why were they called?

2. The Lord always sends his disciples to preach the word of God. In Doctrine and Covenants 42:6, he describes the manner in which they do this. As a minister for the Lord, you are compared or likened unto _____.

3. How does Mormon identify himself in regard to his calling? 3 Nephi 5:13.

4. How did Mormon feel about his son Moroni's calling? Moroni 8:2.

5. Alma the younger was full of joy, as described in Alma 29:9–10. What was his glory? What was his purpose?

6. In Doctrine and Covenants 1:4, the Lord describes a particular duty of the disciples of Christ. What is that duty?

7. A disciple of the Lord Jesus Christ should be willing to do what? Doctrine and Covenants 103:27–28.

8. Mosiah 18:9 teaches about some of your primary duties as a member of the Church. Describe those responsibilities.

9. In Section 84:87–88, the Lord tells you to _____ the world. When people receive you, who will be with you?

10. We preach of _____. 2 Nephi 25:26.

11. What holy calling does Alma speak of in Alma 29:13?

12. Missionaries are to preach the _____. 3 Nephi 20:30.

13. Alma preached _____ and _____. Mosiah 25:15.

14. As a disciple of Christ, you are described in Doctrine and Covenants 103:9–10 as a light. Who is the light? 3 Nephi 18:24; 15:12.

15. What do men do with a candlestick? 3 Nephi 12:15.

16. The Lords calls you the salt of the earth. Matthew 5:13. What causes the salt to become worthless? What is savour?

As you can see, the scriptures teach that you are accountable for taking the gospel to the world. As a disciple of the Lord, you are an instrument in his hands, even an ambassador, a representative of Christ to preach the word, testify of the Father and the Savior, and help your brothers and sisters come unto Christ. The Savior will assist you by the power of his Spirit, and you will partake of the great joy in building up the kingdom of God.

THINGS TO DO

1. Share a copy of the Book of Mormon with a nonmember friend.

2. Commit to prepare to serve your mission and make a plan of preparation.

3. Teach with the missionaries.

4. Set a date to have someone ready to receive the gospel.

5. Read the following statements by the prophets. Then underline or highlight important points.

Ezra Taft Benson: "Why does the Mormon Church continue to send missionaries out into the world, particularly to Christian countries?" May I read the words of the First Presidency of this Church, . . . in which they gave answer to this question. "It is our duty, divinely imposed, to continue urgently and militantly to carry forward our missionary work. We must continue to call missionaries and send them out to preach the gospel, which was never more needed than now, which is the only remedy for the tragic ills that now afflict the world, and which alone can bring peace and brotherly love back amongst the peoples of the earth."
   —Conference Report, April 1942, p. 91.

Ezra Taft Benson: As members of the Lord's Church, we must take missionary work more seriously. The Lord's commission to "preach the gospel to every creature" (Mark 16:15) will never change in our dispensation. We have been greatly blessed with the material means, the technology, and an inspired message to bring the gospel to all men. More is expected of us than any previous generation. Where "much is given much is required." (D&C 82:3.)
   —"Our Responsibility to Share the Gospel," *Ensign,* May 1985, p. 6.

Ezra Taft Benson: Our members need to understand their responsibility to do missionary work and then do it. I fully endorse the words of President Spencer W. Kimball: "Do we really believe in revelation? Then why cannot we accept fully as the revealed word of God the revelation of the Prophet-President David O. McKay, wherein he brought to the Church and to the world this valuable Church slogan, 'Every member a missionary'? How else could the Lord expect to perform His work except through the Saints who have convenanted to serve Him? You and I have made such a covenant. Will we honor our sacred covenant?" (Regional Representatives Seminar, Salt Lake City, Utah, 30 September 1977.)
   As a Church, we have not yet caught that vision. Members are not bringing several hundred thousand members into the Church each year. We have not yet met this challenge of a living prophet. We are still on some of these same plateaus.
   —'President Kimball's Vision of Missionary Work," *Ensign,* July 1985, p. 8.

Joseph F. Smith: There can be no greater, or more important calling for men than that in which the Elders of The Church of Jesus Christ of Latter-day Saints are engaged, when in the discharge of their duties as missionaries to the world. They stand as teachers, counselors and leaders to the people. They are commissioned with the word of life, and "the power of God unto salvation," to minister unto this proud, conceited, self-righteous, but benighted and degenerate world.
   —"The Sacredness of Our Calling," *Millennial Star,* 28 June 1875, p. 408.

Joseph Smith: Every man who has a calling to minister to the inhabitants of the world was ordained to that very purpose in the Grand Council of heaven before this world was.

— *History of the Church,* 6:364.

Spencer W. Kimball: A mission is not just a casual thing — it is not an alternative program in the Church. Neither is a mission a matter of choice any more than tithing is a choice, any more than sacrament meeting is a choice, any more than the Word of Wisdom is a choice. Of course, we have our free agency, and the Lord has given us choices. We can do as we please. We can go on a mission or we can remain home. But every normal young man is as much obligated to go on a mission as he is to pay his tithing, attend his meetings, keep the Sabbath day holy, and keep his life spotless and clean.

—"Circles of Exaltation," in *Charge to Religious Educators,* 2nd edition (Salt Lake City: The Church of Jesus Christ of Latter-day Saints, 1982), p. 10.

Joseph Smith: Remember that your business is to preach the Gospel in all humility and meekness, and warn sinners to repent and come to Christ.

Avoid all contentions and vain disputes with men of corrupt minds, who do not desire to know the truth. Remember that "it is a day of warning, and not a day of many words." If they receive not your testimony in one place, flee to another, remembering to cast no reflections, nor throw out any bitter sayings. If you do your duty, it will be just as well with you, as though all men embraced the Gospel.

—*Teachings of the Prophet Joseph Smith,* compiled Joseph Fielding Smith (Salt Lake City: Deseret Book Company, 1976), p. 43.

CHAPTER 3

THE SPIRIT AND YOU

The living prophets and the scriptures teach the importance and blessing of having the comfort and guidance of the Spirit. Being an instrument in the hands of the Lord requires his disciples to be worthy of the Holy Ghost in their lives.

1. When the Savior left the Americas, the people prayed for what they most desired. What was their desire? 3 Nephi 19:9.

2. Through the Holy Ghost, you can be purified and sanctified. How does one receive this? Helaman 3:35.

3. What price do you need to pay on a daily basis to be filled with the Holy Ghost? 3 Nephi 12:6.

4. To avoid being a natural man or an unrepentant enemy of God, what must you do? Mosiah 3:19.

5. The blessings and fruits of the Spirit are numerous. List them. Doctrine and Covenants 11:12–13; Galatians 5:22–23.

6. The gifts of the Spirit are to profit and bless people. Identify the gifts listed either in Moroni 10:8–17 or Doctrine and Covenants 46:17–27.

7. The power of the Holy Ghost comes by _____. 1 Nephi 10:17.

8. According to Doctrine and Covenants 76:116, what does the Lord require of you to bless you with the Holy Ghost?

9. What must you do for God to give you the Holy Ghost? Acts 5:32.

10. In John 14:26, the Holy Ghost is called the _____. There are many reasons why the Spirit is called this. For instance, it fills you with _____. Moroni 8:26. It tells you _____. Doctrine and Covenants 31:11. In these things you can see the goodness of God in granting you the gifts of the Holy Ghost.

11. The words of Christ are spoken by the _____. 2 Nephi 32:3.

12. Whatever you speak when moved upon by the Holy Ghost is _____, _____, _____, and _____ of the Lord and the _____ to salvation. Doctrine and Covenants 68:3–4.

13. The Holy Ghost will show you _____. 2 Nephi 32:5.

14. The Holy Ghost carries the word _____. 2 Nephi 33:1.

15. Describe the blessings given by the Holy Ghost as identified in the following scriptures.

John 14:26.

John 15:26; 1 Corinthians 12:3; 2 Nephi 31:18.

John 16:13–14.

Romans 5:5.

Romans 14:17.

2 Peter 1:21.

Alma 5:46; Doctrine and Covenants 8:2.

Moroni 10:5.

Doctrine and Covenants 45:57.

16. How can you lose the Spirit? The following scriptures describe this great loss. List the reasons.

2 Nephi 33:2.

Mosiah 2:36.

Helaman 4:24.

Mormon 1:14.

Doctrine and Covenants 42:23; 63:16.

The blessings of having the Holy Ghost in your life are enormous. It will lead, guide, enlighten, show, bless, teach, comfort, testify, witness to, and literally purify you. In your life as a missionary, you *cannot* succeed in any phase of work without the Holy Ghost. You cannot teach (see D&C 42:14; 50:17–22) or be directed in the work.

So living by the Spirit becomes your quest and your goal. Be sure to live worthily so that you do not withdraw from its presence.

THINGS TO DO

1. Identify the moments in the last week when you felt the Spirit. Refer to Doctrine and Covenants 11:12–13; Galations 5:22.

2. Make a list of times when the Spirit gave you the desire to do good. Organize a plan to do good.

3. Pray to live worthy of the blessings of the Spirit.

4. Read the following statements by the prophets. Then underline or highlight important points.

Spencer W. Kimball: As a vital link in the conversion process, we should bear our testimonies that the gospel is true; our testimonies may well be the spark that ignites the conversion process. Consequently, we have a double responsibility: we must testify of the things we know, feel, and have felt, and we must live so the Holy Ghost can be with us and convey our words in power to the heart of the investigator.
    —*Teachings of Spencer W. Kimball,* p. 138.

Ezra Taft Benson: A missionary should never permit himself to see a movie or [read] cheap literature, or hear music that tends to interfere with or which dampens the spirit of missionary work. There is ample evidence that rock music is offensive to the Spirit and affects adversely the spirituality of the missionaries and thus the success of the proselyting work.
    —*The Teachings of Ezra Taft Benson* (Salt Lake City: Bookcraft, 1988), p. 202.

M. Russell Ballard: When the Spirit is present, people are not offended when you share your feelings about the gospel.
    —Conference Report, October 1986, p. 41.

Brigham Young: I had only travelled a short time to testify to the people, before I learned this one fact, that you might prove doctrine from the Bible till doomsday, and it would merely convince a people, but would not convert them. You might read the Bible from Genesis to Revelations, and prove every iota that you advance, and that alone would have no converting influence upon the people. Nothing short of a testimony by the power of the Holy Ghost would bring light and knowledge to them—bring them in their hearts to repentance. Nothing short of that would ever do.
    —*Journal of Discourses,* 5:327.

Joseph Smith: The Elders would go forth, and each must stand for himself . . . to go in all meekness, in sobriety, and preach Jesus Christ and Him crucified; not to contend with others on account of their faith, or systems of religion, but pursue a steady course. This I delivered by way of commandment; and all who observe it not, will pull down persecution upon their heads, while those who do, shall always be filled with the Holy Ghost; this I pronounced as a prophecy, and sealed with hosanna and amen.

—*History of the Church*, 2:431.

Ezra Taft Benson: A missionary who is inspired by the Spirit of the Lord must be led by that Spirit to choose the proper approach to be effective. We must not forget that the Lord Himself provided the Book of Mormon as His chief witness. The Book of Mormon is still our most powerful missionary tool. Let us use it.

—*Teachings of Ezra Taft Benson*, p. 204.

Ezra Taft Benson: Be guided by the Spirit. I have said so many times to my Brethren that the Spirit is the most important single element in this work. With the Spirit, and by magnifying your call, you can do miracles for the Lord in the mission field. Without the Spirit you will never succeed regardless of your talent and ability.

—*Teachings of Ezra Taft Benson*, p. 205.

John A. Widtsoe: The gift of the Holy Ghost confers upon a person the right to receive, as he may desire and need, the presence, light and intelligence of the Holy Ghost. It gives, as it were, an official claim upon the mighty assistance and comforting assurance of the Holy Ghost. When the servants of the Lord display a spiritual power beyond the command of man; when the grief-laden heart beats with joy; when failure is converted into victory, it is by the visitation of the Holy Ghost. It is the Spirit of God under the direction of the Holy Ghost that quickeneth all things.

The gift of the Holy Ghost remains inoperative unless a person leads a blameless life. Worthiness determines whether a person shall enjoy the privileges promised when the "gift" is conferred. It is useless to expect this high official assistance unless there is daily conformity to the laws of the gospel. Faith and prayer, out of the heart and unceasing, will fit a person for the presence of the Holy Ghost, and to such a life he will respond in power.

Latter-day Saints have received, under the hands of those divinely empowered, this inexpressibly glorious "gift," which will lead them if they are fitted, into the companionship of the Holy Ghost, and win for them intelligence and power to win joy in life and exaltation in the world to come. Those who have been so blessed have not always understood the greatness of that which has been given them, or have not earnestly sought its help. So powerful a gift, with such boundless promise, justifies every attempt to cleanse body and soul. Certain it is, that only with the aid of the Holy Ghost shall we be able to rise to the heights of salvation of which we dream and for which we pray.

—*Man and the Dragon* (Salt Lake City: Bookcraft, 1945), pp. 150–51.

President Ezra Taft Benson: To be a successful missionary one must have the Spirit of the Lord. We are also taught that the Spirit will not dwell in unclean tabernacles. Therefore, one of the first things a missionary must do to gain spirituality is to make sure his own personal life is in order.

—*Teachings of Ezra Taft Benson*, pp. 198–99.

PERSONAL WORTHINESS

FAITH UNTO REPENTANCE THROUGH
THE ATONEMENT OF CHRIST

FASTING AND PRAYER

INTEGRITY AND SACRIFICE

YOUR ATTITUDE AND SELF-RESPECT

CHARITY

OBEDIENCE

CHAPTER 4

FAITH UNTO REPENTANCE THROUGH THE ATONEMENT OF CHRIST

In order to teach faith unto repentance, you must live faith unto repentance through applying the atonement of Christ to your life—thus bringing a change of heart. What does that involve?

1. Alma 34:15–17 describes what one must do to obtain mercy in the great plan of redemption. Describe what each person must do.

2. How will we suffer if we don't repent? Doctrine and Covenants 19:15–20.

3. Who is an enemy to God? Mosiah 2:36–38.

4. To repent of your sins, you must _____ and _____. Doctrine and Covenants 58:43.

5. What is the Lord's blessing when you repent? Doctrine and Covenants 58:42.

6. What happened when Enos pleaded for forgiveness? Enos 1:5–8.

7. Summarize Alma 7:14–16.

8. What are some of the behaviors that follow the repentance of people? Alma 14:1; Enos 1:9, 11.

9. What does Alma 34:32–35 caution you to do?

10. What are some of the blessings described in Alma 26:22 concerning those who repent and exercise faith?

11. Remember, repentance and forgiveness are not one-time occurrences. What does the Lord say about this in Mosiah 26:30 and Moroni 6:8?

12. If we believe in Christ, what will we do? Helaman 14:13.

13. True repentance is always accompanied by _____. Matthew 3:8; Acts 26:20; Helaman 12:24.

14. How do you know when repentance is fulfilled in forgiveness? Enos 1:5–6; Mosiah 27:28–29; 3 Nephi 27:20.

Faith and repentance are mentioned over one thousand times in the scriptures. Faith is the foundation of all righteousness. Faith is hoping for things *not seen*, which are true. Faith is the moving cause of all action. Faith is power to do all things, and faith is the power of the priesthood. Faith is required of everyone in order to please God. For these reasons, missionaries are commanded to teach faith and repentance. As you become meek and lowly, you can increase faith through (1) hearing the word of God, (2) praying and fasting and (3) increasing your love and righteousness—remembering that faith is a gift of God. The greatest blessing in one's life is the power that faith gives, even *faith unto repentance*. That is, faith in Jesus Christ, leading to repentance through Jesus Christ. For the new disciple, that means accepting baptism and *taking upon oneself the name* of Jesus Christ. For the baptized disciples that means renewing one's baptism and baptismal covenants through the sacrament.

The principles and ordinances of the gospel apply the Atonement directly to your life. Repentance becomes the greatest thing you will ever do in regard to exaltation. The joy that Alma described concerning his repentance explains why he wanted all to taste of the joy he felt. Everyone can repent—recognize their sins, have Godly sorrow, confess their sins, forsake them, make restitution (as far as he or she is able, trusting in the strength and power of Christ's atonement to make up for the rest), and forgive others.

As you go and do good works, let the words of King Benjamin sink deep into your heart: "Believe that ye must repent of your sins and forsake them, and humble yourselves before God; and ask in sincerity of heart that he would forgive you; and now, if you believe all these things see that you do them.

"And again . . . as ye have come to the knowledge of the glory of God, or if ye have known of his goodness and have tasted of his love, and have received a remission of your sins, which causeth such exceedingly great joy in your souls, even so I would that ye should remember, and always retain in remembrance, the greatness of God, and your own nothingness, and his goodness and long-suffering towards you, unworthy creatures, and humble yourselves even in the depths of humility, calling on the name of the Lord daily, and standing steadfastly in the faith of that which is to come, which was spoken by the mouth of the angel. . . .

"If you do this ye shall always rejoice, and be filled with the love of God, and always retain a remission of your sins; and ye shall grow in the knowledge of the glory of him that created you, or in the knowledge of that which is just and true. And ye will not have a mind to injure one another, but to live peaceably, and to render to every man according to that which is his due." (Mosiah 4:10–13.)

THINGS TO DO

1. Read 2 Nephi 9:4–12, 25–26; Alma 34:8–16; 42:1–15, 23–24; and Doctrine and Covenants 19:15–20; and make a list of the blessings from the Atonement.

2. Read Enos 1:1–10.

3. Consider what you can do to increase your faith in Jesus Christ, which leads to repentance.

   a. When should I repent?

   b. How often should I repent?

4. If there is a moral concern, *talk to your bishop now.*

5. Make a commitment to live worthy to serve an honorable mission.

6. Read the scriptures listed under the topics of faith and repentance in the Topical Guide in the LDS edition of the Bible.

7. Read the following statements by the prophets. Then underline or highlight important points.

Joseph Fielding Smith: May I say, as plainly and as forcefully as I can, that we believe in Christ. We accept him without reservation as the Son of God and the Savior of the world.

We believe that he came into the world to ransom men from the temporal and spiritual death brought into the world through the fall of Adam, and we have in our hearts unbounded gratitude that through the shedding of his blood all men are raised in immortality, while those who believe and obey his laws are raised also unto eternal life.

We believe that salvation was, and is, and is to come in and through the atoning blood of Christ, the Lord Omnipotent, and that there is no other name given under heaven whereby men can become inheritors of eternal glory in the kingdoms which are ahead.

—"The First Prophet of the Last Dispensation," *Ensign*, August 1971, p. 6.

James E. Talmage: The structure of the word [*atonement*] in its present form is suggestive of the true meaning; it is literally *at-one-ment*, "denoting reconciliation, or the bringing into agreement of those who have been estranged." And such is the significance of the saving sacrifice of the Redeemer, whereby He expiated the transgression of the fall, through which death came into the world, and provided ready and efficient means for man's attainment of immortality through reconciliation with God.

—*The Articles of Faith*, revised pag. and typog. (Salt Lake City: Deseret Book Company, 1983), p. 68.

Joseph Smith: Notwithstanding the transgression, by which man had cut himself off from an immediate intercourse with his Maker without a Mediator, it appears that the great and glorious plan of His redemption was previously provided; the sacrifice prepared; the atonement wrought out in the mind and purpose of God, even in the person of the Son, through whom man was now to look for acceptance and through whose merits he was now taught that he alone could find redemption, since the word had been pronounced, Unto dust thou shalt return.

But that man was not able himself to erect a system, or plan with power sufficient to free him from a destruction which awaited him is evident from the fact that God, as before remarked, prepared a sacrifice in the gift of His own Son who should be sent in due time, to prepare a way, or open a door through which man might enter into the Lord's presence, whence he had been cast out for disobedience.

—*Teachings of the Prophet Joseph Smith*, pp. 57–58.

Joseph F. Smith: When we commit sin, it is necessary that we repent of it and make restitution as far as lies in our power. When we cannot make restitution for the wrong we have done, then we must apply for the grace and mercy of God to cleanse us from that iniquity.

Men cannot forgive their own sins; they cannot cleanse themselves from the consequences of their sins. Men can stop sinning and can do right in the future, and so far their acts are acceptable before the Lord and worthy of consideration. But who shall repair the wrongs they have done to themselves and to others, which it seems impossible for them to repair themselves? By the atonement of Jesus Christ the sins of the repentant shall be washed away; though they be crimson they shall be made white as wool. This is the promise given to you. We who have not paid our tithing in the past, and are therefore under obligations to the Lord, which we are not in position to discharge, the Lord requires that no longer at our hands, but will forgive us for the past if we will observe this law honestly in the future. That is generous and kind, and I feel grateful for it.

—*Gospel Doctrine,* 5th edition (Salt Lake City: Deseret Book Company, 1939), pp. 98–99.

James E. Talmage: Christ gave His life willingly and voluntarily for the redemption of mankind. He had offered Himself, in the primeval council in heaven, as the subject of the atoning sacrifice made necessary by the foreseen transgression of the first man; and the free agency shown and exercised in this, the early stage of His saving mission, was retained to the very last of the agonizing fulfilment of the accepted plan.

—*Articles of Faith,* p. 71.

Joseph Fielding Smith: Jesus is the only person born into this world who did not have an earthly father. The Father of his body is also the Father of his Spirit, and the Father of the spirits of all men. From his Father he obtained eternal life; from his mother he obtained the power to die, for his mother was a mortal woman. From her he got his blood, and from his Father he got his immortality. Thus having the power to lay down his life and take it again, he was able to pay the price of Adam's transgression, and redeem all creatures from the grave.

—*Answers to Gospel Questions,* compiled Joseph Fielding Smith, Jr., 5 vols. (Salt Lake City: Deseret Book Company, 1957–66), 2:136.

Joseph Fielding Smith: We get into the habit of thinking, I suppose, that his great suffering was when he was nailed to the cross by his hands and his feet and was left there to suffer until he died. As excruciating as that pain was, that was not the greatest suffering that he had to undergo, for in some way which I cannot understand, but which I accept on faith, and which you must accept on faith, he carried on his back the burden of the sins of the whole world. It is hard enough for me to carry my own sins. How is it with you? And yet he had to carry the sins of the whole world, as our Savior and the Redeemer of a fallen world, and so great was his suffering before he ever went to the cross, we are informed, that blood oozed from the pores of his body, and he prayed to his Father that the cup might pass if it were possible, but not being possible he was willing to drink.

—Conference Report, October 1947, pp. 147–48.

Spencer W. Kimball: There are many people who seem to rely solely on the Lord's mercy rather than on accomplishing their own repentance. One woman rather flippantly said, "The Lord knows my intents and that I'd like to give up my bad habits. He will understand and forgive me." But the scriptures will not bear this out. The Lord may temper justice with mercy, but he will never supplant it. Mercy can never replace justice. God is *merciful,* but he is also *just.* The Savior's atonement represents the mercy extended. Because of this atonement, all men can be saved. Most men can be exalted.

Many have greatly misunderstood the place of mercy in the forgiveness program. Its role is not to give great blessings without effort. Were it not for the atonement of

Christ, the shedding of his blood, the assumption by proxy of our sins, man could never be forgiven and cleansed. Justice and mercy work hand in hand. Having offered mercy to us in the overall redemption, the Lord must now let justice rule, for he cannot save us in our sins.

—*Miracle of Forgiveness* (Salt Lake City: Bookcraft, 1969), pp. 358–59.

John Taylor: Transgression of the law brought death upon all the posterity of Adam, the restoration through the atonement restored all the human family to life. "For since by man came death, by man came also the resurrection of the dead. For as in Adam all die, even so in Christ shall all be made alive." So that whatever was lost by Adam, was restored by Jesus Christ.

The penalty of the transgression of the law was the death of the body. The atonement made by Jesus Christ resulted in the resurrection of the human body. Its scope embraced all peoples, nations and tongues. . . .

This is one part of the restoration.

—*The Mediation and Atonement* (Salt Lake City: Deseret News Company, 1882), pp. 178–79.

Marion G. Romney: There is another phase of the atonement which makes me love the Savior even more, and fills my soul with gratitude beyond expression. It is that in addition to atoning for Adam's transgression, thereby bringing about the resurrection, the Savior by his suffering paid the debt for my personal sins. He paid the debt for your personal sins and for the personal sins of every living soul that ever dwelt upon the earth or that ever will dwell in mortality upon the earth. But this he did conditionally. The benefits of this suffering for our individual transgressions will not come to us unconditionally in the same sense that the resurrection will come regardless of what we do. If we partake of the blessings of the atonement as far as our individual transgressions are concerned, we must obey the law.

—Conference Report, October 1953, p. 35.

John Taylor: Though others might be the sons of God through Him, yet it needed His body, His fulfilment of the law, the sacrifice or offering up of that body in the atonement, before any of these others, who were also sons of God by birth in the spirit world, could attain to the position of sons of God as He was; and that only through His mediation and atonement. So that in Him, and of Him, and through Him, through the principle of adoption, could we alone obtain that position which is spoken of by John: "Beloved, now are we the sons of God; and it doth not yet appear what we shall be: but we know that when he shall appear we shall be like him, for we shall see him as he is." [1 John 3:2.] Thus His atonement made it possible for us to obtain an exaltation, which we could not have possessed without it.

—*The Mediation and Atonement*, pp. 137–38.

Joseph Fielding Smith: A man walking along the road happens to fall into a pit so deep and dark that he cannot climb to the surface and regain his freedom. How can he save himself from his predicament? Not by any exertions on his part, for there is no means of escape in the pit. He calls for help and some kindly disposed soul, hearing his cries for relief, hastens to his assistance and by lowering a ladder, gives to him the means by which he may climb again to the surface of the earth.

This was precisely the condition that Adam placed himself and his posterity in, when he partook of the forbidden fruit. All being together in the pit, none could gain the surface and relieve the others. The pit was banishment from the presence of the

Lord and temporal death, the dissolution of the body. And all being subject to death, none could provide the means of escape. Therefore, in his infinite mercy, the Father heard the cries of his children and sent his Only Begotten Son, who was not subject to death nor to sin, to provide the means of escape. This he did through his infinite atonement and the everlasting gospel.

—*Doctrines of Salvation,* compiled Bruce R. McConkie, 3 volumes (Salt Lake City: Bookcraft, 1954–56), 1:126–27.

Brigham Young: The moment the atonement of the Savior is done away, that moment, at one sweep, the hopes of salvation entertained by the Christian world are destroyed, the foundation of their faith is taken away, and there is nothing left for them to stand upon. When it is gone all the revelations God ever gave to the Jewish nation, to the Gentiles, and to us are rendered valueless, and all hope is taken from us at one sweep.

—*Discourses of Brigham Young,* selected John A. Widtsoe (Salt Lake City: Deseret Book Company, 1941), p. 27.

Joseph Fielding Smith: What a dreadful situation we would have been in without this infinite atonement! Our bodies returning to the dust there to remain forever; our spirits becoming subject to Satan, and we would have had no recourse. How grateful we should be for the mercies of our Eternal Father and his beloved Son that the way was opened for our escape.

—*Answers to Gospel Questions,* 2:138.

Bruce R. McConkie: Baptism is a new birth; it is symbolical of our new life in the kingdom of God, which new birth is a living reality because of the shedding of the blood of Christ, or in other words because of his death, burial, and resurrection. The new birth grows out of the atonement wrought by our Lord; the newness of life comes to the repentant sinner because he has bowed to the will of the Lord and has been immersed in water by a legal administrator. Paul states it this way: "Know ye not, that so many of us as were baptized into Jesus Christ were baptized into his death?" That is, even as Christ died on the cross, so we die in baptism. "Therefore we are buried with him by baptism into death." Dead people are buried, Christ in the Arimathean's tomb, every baptized person in a watery grave. But death is not eternal, and "like as Christ was raised up from the dead by the glory of the Father, even so we also should walk in newness of life." That is to say: 'Glory be to the Father by whose almighty power our Lord rose from the dead; he took up his body again in glorious immortality; the resurrection became a reality; he lived again. And even so, every baptized person, coming forth from the water, lives again in a newness of life.' "For if we have been planted together in the likeness of his death, we shall be also in the likeness of his resurrection: Knowing this, that our old man is crucified with him, that the body of sin might be destroyed, that henceforth we should not serve sin." Sometimes the spiritual struggle to slay sin, that the new convert may be free therefrom, is as savage a warfare as death by crucifixion. But when sin is destroyed in our lives, it is no longer our master. We are "dead indeed unto sin, but alive unto God through Jesus Christ our Lord." (Rom. 6:3–11.)

—*The Promised Messiah* (Salt Lake City: Deseret Book Company, 1978), pp. 389–90.

Bruce R. McConkie: This Church administers the gospel and offers salvation to all who will believe in Christ and live his laws.

What is the fulness of the everlasting gospel? It is the plan of salvation—the Father's eternal plan to save his children.

It is the begetting of spirit children, the teachings and testings of our premortal existence, the creation of worlds without number, and (for us) our inheritance here on planet earth.

It is the fall of Adam, with its temporal and spiritual death, and the ransoming power of the Son of God, who abolished death and brought life and immortality to light through his laws.

It is all of the laws, rites, and ordinances; all of the truths, powers, and performances; all of the keys, priesthoods, and privileges which bring to pass the immortality and eternal life of man.

It is the atonement of Christ, the redemption of man, the opening of the graves, the wonder and glory of eternal life.

It is faith, repentance, and baptism; it is the gifts of the Spirit, the revelations of heaven, and the unspeakable gift of the Holy Ghost.

It is eternal marriage and eternal lives and eternal exaltation. It is to be one with the Father and the Son and to reign with them forever on their throne.

It is the tests and trials of this mortal probation; it is sorrow and pain and death; it is overcoming the world and pursuing a godly course in spite of earth and hell; it is keeping the commandments and serving our fellowmen.

And, finally, it is to sit down with Abraham, Isaac, and Jacob, and all the holy prophets, in the kingdom of God to go no more out.

—"This Final Glorious Gospel Dispensation," *Ensign,* April 1980, p. 21.

Brigham Young: Now, my brethren, you who have sinned, repent of your sins. I can say to you in regard to Jesus and the atonement (it is so written, and I firmly believe it), that Christ has died for all. He has paid the full debt, whether you receive the gift or not. But if we continue to sin, to lie, steal, bear false witness, we must repent of and forsake that sin to have the full efficacy of the blood of Christ. Without this it will be of no effect; repentance must come, in order that the atonement may prove a benefit to us.

—*Journal of Discourses,* 11:375.

CHAPTER 5

FASTING AND PRAYER

Fasting and prayer will bring the power of God into your life and into the lives of the people whom you seek to bless. You must learn self-mastery and increase in your spirituality so that you can be a worthy instrument to bless others.

1. Your Heavenly Father has continuously asked you to call upon him in mighty prayer. Summarize James 1:5–6.

2. Fasting and prayer are coupled in the following scriptures. List the blessings each scripture identifies.

   Alma 5:46.

   Alma 6:6.

   Alma 17:3.

   Alma 17:9.

   Helaman 3:35.

3 Nephi 27:1–2.

3. What do you learn about fasting and prayer in Doctrine and Covenants 88:76?

4. What words are used to describe Enos's prayer in Enos 1:1–4? What do they suggest about the effort that goes into prayer?

5. What was required of Alma the elder's and the people's prayers in order that they could be answered? Mosiah 27:13–14.

6. What does 2 Nephi 32:8–9 teach about the importance of prayer?

7. 3 Nephi 20:1 teaches to always pray in your _____.
8. To receive the pure love of Christ, how should you pray? Moroni 7:48.

9. The following scriptures from the Doctrine and Covenants list specific blessings of prayer. List them.
   31:12.

   42:14.

   46:7.

46:30.

52:9.

75:11.

84:61.

108:7.

10. Doctrine and Covenants 67:10 lists two things you must rid yourself of in order to know God. List them and then write down how you can overcome them. What is the third quality you must develop?

You can see that the blessings of fasting and prayer are abundant. Fasting and prayer can bring you knowledge and testimony of God, the love of Christ, the Spirit, and answers to expedient concerns; they can bring you added strength, deliver you from temptation, give you power to do all things, and help you endure to the end. In fine, they allow you the privilege of communicating better with your Heavenly Father.

THINGS TO DO

1. Fast and pray for the following:
   • faith and repentance—Alma 34:16–17
   • the pure love of Christ—Moroni 7:47–48
   • humility and faith—Helaman 3:35
   • the welfare of the Saints—Moroni 6:5
   • to teach with power and authority of God—Alma 17:3
   • to know the truth of all things—Moroni 10:5

2. Read the following statements by the prophets. Then underline or highlight important points.

John Taylor: I will tell you the first thing I used to do when I went preaching, particularly when I went to a fresh place—and that was to go aside to some place, anywhere I could get, into a field, a barn, into the woods, or my closet, and ask God to bless me and give me wisdom to meet all the circumstances with which I might have to contend; and the Lord gave me the wisdom I needed and sustained me. If you pursue a course of this kind, he will bless you also.

—*The Gospel Kingdom: Selections from the Writings and Discourses of John Taylor* (Salt Lake City: Bookcraft, 1987), p. 240.

David O. McKay: Prayer is the pulsation of a yearning, loving heart in tune with the Infinite. It is a message of the soul sent directly to a loving Father. The language is not mere words but spirit vibration.

—*Treasures of Life,* compiled Clare Middlemiss (Salt Lake City: Deseret Book Company, 1962), p. 308.

Brigham Young: I would like to impress upon the minds of the brethren, that he who goes forth in the name of the Lord, trusting in Him with all his heart, will never want for wisdom to answer any question that is asked him, or to give any counsel that may be required to lead the people in the way of life and salvation, and he will never be confounded worlds without end. . . . Go in the name of the Lord, trust in the name of the Lord, lean upon the Lord, and call upon the Lord fervently and without ceasing, and pay no attention to the world.

—*Journal of Discourses,* 12:34.

Ezra Taft Benson: Your greatest help will come from the Lord Himself as you supplicate and plead with Him in humble prayer. As you are driven to your knees again and again, asking Him for divine help in your mission, you will feel the Spirit, you will get your answer from above, your mission will prosper spiritually because of your dependence and your reliance on Him. . . . The modern-day challenging and testifying missionary prays every morning to "lead me this day to a family that I can fulfil my purpose."

—*Teachings of Ezra Taft Benson,* pp. 199–200.

Neal A. Maxwell: It is both proper and important for us in our afflictions and trials to ask for relief through fasting, prayer, and priesthood blessings. But after all we can do, we then submit to God's will as did Jesus in Gethsemane and on the cross, when, in anguish, He posed aloud the possibility that the cup might pass from Him. On that occasion, the key word that expressed Jesus' attribute of submissiveness was "nevertheless."

—*Even As I Am* (Salt Lake City: Deseret Book Company, 1982), p. 47.

Joseph F. Smith: I say to my brethren, when they are fasting, and praying for the sick, and for those that need faith and prayer, do not go beyond what is wise and prudent in fasting and prayer. The Lord can hear a simple prayer, offered in faith, in half a dozen words, and he will recognize fasting that may not continue more than twenty-four hours, just as readily and as effectually as He will answer a prayer of a thousand words and fasting for a month.

—Conference Report, October 1912, pp. 133–34.

Delbert L. Stapley: [Fasting and prayer are] a source of strength, a source of power, a source of blessing that perhaps as a people we are not using enough; that it does have tremendous spiritual value to those who observe the law, and who apply it faithfully. It also seems to me that fasting and prayer can be employed to bless others, and if we would faithfully observe the law, the blessings of our Heavenly Father would collectively be given to the people of the Church.

    —Conference Report, October 1951, p. 122.

Wilford Woodruff: We should call upon the Lord in mighty prayer, and make all our wants known unto Him. For if He does not protect and deliver us and save us, no other power will. Therefore our trust is entirely in Him. Therefore our prayers should ascend into the ears of our heavenly Father day and night.

    —"An Epistle from the President of the Twelve Apostles," *Millennial Star,* 20 December 1886, p. 806.

CHAPTER 6

INTEGRITY AND SACRIFICE

Integrity is the quality of wholeness, of being undivided in your adherance to moral values. It makes you sincere, upright, and honest to the depths of your soul. Integrity coupled with sacrifice brings about a worthiness and qualification for the work. To sacrifice is to act or offer oneself for the sake of a higher value or service by forgoing your own interest. You literally give up your "comfort" for the welfare of the kingdom of God, which, of course, is composed of the children of God.

1. The Lord expressed his love for Hyrum. What did he praise Hyrum for? Doctrine and Covenants 124:15.

2. Isaiah 29:13 teaches us that integrity is more than lip service. What was the problem Isaiah identified?

3. Proverbs 20:7 states, "The just man walketh in his _____." What other blessing is noted?

4. Men are sometimes unstable in their ways; they are inconsistent. James 1:8 describes a man of this nature as being _____.

5. The Ammonites exemplified truly converted people. Describe their behavior as noted in Alma 27:27.

6. In asking the Lord for blessings or answers to prayer, Moroni 10:4 and Doctrine and Covenants 8:1 suggest that a person have a certain kind of heard. What two qualities are mentioned?

7. Article of Faith 13 describes the character of a Latter-day Saint. List four to five attributes one should seek to possess.

8. Psalm 50:5 and Doctrine and Covenants 97:8 describe a way you can covenant with the Lord. According to these scriptures, what do you do?

9. Omni 1:26 describes an offering to the Lord. What is that offering?

10. In making your soul pure before the Lord, you are commanded in 3 Nephi 9:20 to offer a certain kind of sacrifice to the Lord. Describe your sacrifice.

11. With what kind of sacrifices is God well pleased? Hebrews 13:15–16.

12. Sacrifice often involves a choice—choosing something rather than something else. What does the Lord admonish you to seek and to not seek? Matthew 6:33 (note the JST in the footnotes).

When integrity becomes part of your character, and when you sacrifice for the kingdom of God, your worthiness to be an instrument will increase to such a point that you will be endowed with blessings from on high. (See Helaman 10:4–5.) As you give your heart to the Lord, your mind, your decisions, your affections, and even your very soul come under his influence and direction. This integrity of heart makes sacrifice a logical step in becoming Christlike. You sacrifice your own desires for the Lord. You put Heavenly Father first in your life. You seek to build up the kingdom of God. You ensure your covenants through faithful obedience and sacrifice. Because your heart is pure, sincere, and upright before the Lord, sacrifice truly brings forth the blessings of heaven now and throughout the eternities.

THINGS TO DO

1. To better understand the meaning of sacrifice, give up something you enjoy (a food, an activity, etc.) and use the money or time for something good.

2. Practice speaking and behaving with *exact* honesty.

3. Think of the commitments and covenants you have made and evaluate your performance and integrity regarding them.

4. Read the following statements by the prophets. Then underline or highlight important points.

James E. Faust: Disciples follow the Divine Master. Their actions speak in symphonic harmony with their beliefs. They know who they are. They know what God expects of them. They mirror inner peace and certainty concerning the mission and resurrection of Christ. They hunger and thirst after righteousness. They know they are here on this earth for a purpose. They understand life after death.

They believe that the transcendent event in the ministry of the Christ was the Atonement, culminating in the Resurrection.

—Conference Report, April 1985, p. 38.

ElRay L. Christiansen: Missionary service is not only a test of *faith* but a *real* test of *character*.

—Conference Report, April 1959, p. 13.

Spencer W. Kimball: *Integrity* may be defined as a quality of being complete, unbroken, whole, and unimpaired purity and moral soundness; it is unadulterated genuineness and deep sincerity. *It is honesty and righteousness.*

Some people keep scrupulously clean their bodies, teeth, hair, and clothes, but permit their morals to degenerate. . . . Practically all dishonesty owes its existence and growth to this inward distortion we call *self-justification.* It is the first, the worst, and most insidious and damaging form of cheating—to cheat oneself.

—Mexico and Central America Area Conference Report, 1972, p. 27.

John Taylor: There is one great principle by which, I think, we all of us ought to be actuated in our worship, above everything else that we are associated with in life, and that is honesty of purpose. . . .

It is proper that men should be honest with themselves, that they should be honest with each other in all their words, dealings, intercourse, intercommunication, business arrangements, and everything else. They ought to be governed by truthfulness, honesty, and integrity, and that man is very foolish indeed who would not be true to himself, true to his convictions and feelings in regard to religious matters.

—*The Gospel Kingdom,* p. 231.

YOUR ATTITUDE AND SELF-RESPECT

Your mental perspective of yourself and the work will greatly affect your capacity for service. As Elder Neal A. Maxwell often says, "Have an attitude of gratitude." President Harold B. Lee has also said, "Those lacking in that important understanding [of who they are,] and, consequently, in some degree [those] failing to hold themselves in the high esteem which they would have if they did understand, are lacking self-respect." (Conference Report, October 1973, p. 5.) Your perspective, or attitude, needs to be right, and that is affected by the respect, or lack of it, that you have for yourself. As you come to know your divine nature, capacity, and worth, your attitude will improve, and your self-respect will increase.

1. Psalm 82:6, Acts 17:29, Romans 8:16 all indicate who you are. You are the _____
    _____.

2. When you covenant through baptism, you become the _____. Mosiah 5:7.

3. Because of the Atonement and our divine potential, you can become _____. 3 Nephi 12:48.

4. What does John 3:16–17 teach you about God's love for you and what he has done for you? If you know the depth of God's love for you, you will feel better about yourself and will thus have a more positive attitude.

5. The Lord finds great joy over the souls that _____. Doctrine and Covenants 18:13.

6. Doctrine and Covenants 58:26–28 describes a positive, enthusiastic attitude. What are the results?

7. What was the attitude of the converts that Ammon taught in Alma 21:23?

Having a positive attitude toward life, the Lord's work, and yourself is very important. It sets the stage for every day of your life. Satan's outlook is negative, and he seeks to make you miserable, as he is. (See 2 Nephi 2:18.) The Lord's outlook is positive, and he seeks to fill you with joy. (See Mosiah 4:20.) Recognize and remember the goodness of God, count your many blessings, and look to bless others—these things will help you have a positive attitude.

One day a missionary asked, "President Pinegar, why are you always so happy and positive?" I replied, "I'm my Heavenly Father's boy." That simple fact has helped me all my life. We are all God's children. We are of great worth. We have the capacity to be like our Father. If you remember these things your self-respect will increase. You will choose to serve and bless others, fulfilling your divine role as a child of God.

THINGS TO DO

1. Make a list of positive statements about yourself and your present situation.

2. Make a list of your blessings from the Lord.

3. Choose to smile at people you meet.

4. Read the following statements by the prophets. Then underline or highlight important points.

Spencer W. Kimball: Missionary work benefits from enthusiasm. With such a noble work one should not find it too difficult to develop enthusiasm. Enthusiasm is real interest plus dedicated energy, and this combination provides the most dynamic of all human qualities. But anyone who does not have it naturally can cultivate it by applying autosuggestion. Merely deciding that a job is going to be interesting helps to make it so.
  —*Teachings of Spencer W. Kimball, p. 573.*

Wilford Woodruff: I have waded swamps and swum rivers, and have asked my bread from door to door; and have devoted nearly fifty years to this work. And why? Was there gold enough in California to have hired me to do it? No, verily; and what I have done and what my brethren have done, we have done because we were commanded of God. And this is the position we occupy today. We have preached and labored at home and abroad, and we intend to continue our labors, by the help of God, as long as we can have liberty to do it, and until the Gentiles prove themselves unworthy of eternal life, and until the judgments of God overtake the world, which are at the door.
  —*Journal of Discourses, 23:130.*

Ezra Taft Benson: If you want to keep the Spirit, to love your mission and not be homesick, you must work. But, remember the words of President Thomas S. Monson: "Work without vision is drudgery. Vision without work is dreaming. Work coupled with vision is destiny." There is no greater exhilaration or satisfaction than to know, after a hard day of missionary work, that you have done your best.
  —*Teachings of Ezra Taft Benson, pp. 200–201.*

Ezra Taft Benson: It is so important that you lose yourselves in this work, that you don't worry about "what is it going to do for me." You are not out in the world with self-improvement as the major objective, but you can't help getting a maximum amount of self-improvement if you lose yourself in the work of the Lord. I don't know of any better preparation for life than two years of devoted, unselfish, dedicated service as a missionary.

—*God, Family, Country,* pp. 59–60.

Wilford Woodruff: There never was a set of men since God made the world under a stronger responsibility to warn this generation, to lift up our voices long and loud, day and night so far as we have the opportunity and declare the words of God unto this generation. We are required to do this. This is our calling. It is our duty. It is our business.

—*Journal of Discourses,* 21:122.

George Q. Cannon: I do hope that, as soon as you get into your fields of labor, you will not apologize to the people for your weaknesses, and tell them how incapable and unfitted you are for such positions as you may hold. . . . Go into your fields of labor as men of God, appointed by Him to minister unto them the things pertaining to their salvation, and they will find that you have power which no other men, devoid of the authority you have, possess.

—*Gospel Truth,* compiled Jerreld L. Newquist, 2 vols. (Salt Lake City: Deseret Book Co., 1957), 2:78.

Marvin J. Ashton: To be aware of one's limitations and potentials on a continuing basis will help in improved self-esteem. We need to be constantly aware of the fact that we are children of God. He knows us. He hears us. He loves us. Proper self-image will help us keep our habits, lives, and souls directed in happy paths. . . . To teach self-discipline, the emphasis should be on self-respect and esteem rather than the use of ridicule, embarrassment, and tears for conduct-improvement tools. One of the great tragedies that can come in a human's life is the destruction of self-respect. This destruction is often self-inflicted. Elevated expressions of human feelings, example, and courtesy build self-respect. People are lifted when they are treated as if they already were what they could be. It is my experience that most thinking people respond better to friendly persuasion than to threats or abuse.

—Conference Report, October 1976, p. 126.

Russell M. Nelson: The next prerequisite to joy is to feel good about yourself. The second of our Lord's two great commandments carries a double charge: "Thou shalt love thy neighbour as thyself" (Matthew 22:39). Therefore, love of companion is governed, in part, by esteem of self, and so is joy. . . .

Spiritual *and* physical elements each must be nurtured if we are to earn proper self-esteem. . . . *Spiritual* self-esteem begins with the realization that each new morning is a gift from God. Even the air we breathe is a loving loan from him. He preserves us from day to day and supports us from one moment to another (see Mosiah 2:21). . . .

Joy cometh in the morning—to those who can stand before the mirror and feel clean, to those whose mouths are free from the taste of flavors forbidden by the Lord, to those whose spirits and bodies are free from feelings of self-remorse.

—Conference Report, October 1986, pp. 86, 88.

Thomas S. Monson: At times, all of us let that enemy of achievement—even the culprit, self-defeat—dwarf our aspirations, smother our dreams, cloud our vision, and wreck our lives. The enemy's voice whispers in our ears, "I can't do it." "I'm too little." "Everyone is watching." "I'm nobody." This is when we need to reflect on the counsel of Maxwell Maltz, who declared that "the most . . . realistic self-image of all is to conceive of yourself as 'made in the image of God.' " You cannot sincerely hold this conviction without experiencing a profound new sense of strength and power. (*Psycho-Cybernetics* [Englewood Cliffs, N.J.: Prentice-Hall, 1960], p. 245.)

—Conference Report, April 1989, p. 56.

CHARITY

Possessing the pure love of Christ—called *charity* in the scriptures—will make you not only worthy but also prepare you to share the gospel of Jesus Christ. As you acquire the concern for others that brings about righteous service, your charity increases, and you become motivated to invite all mankind to come unto Christ. There are two facets to charity: (1) Christ's love for you—expressed through the Atonement, and (2) your pure love of Christ—your love for Christ expressed through attributes of Christlikeness that bless others.

1. Moroni explained that the great atonement Christ wrought was based on his love for the children of men. He mentioned this love as being _____. Ether 12:33–34.

2. Charity, then is the pure love of Christ. You are _____ to have charity. 2 Nephi 26:30.

3. What are you without charity? Moroni 7:44, 46.

4. What do charity and love do for you?
   Moroni 10:20–21.

Moroni 7:47.

Doctrine and Covenants 4:5.

41

Moroni 8:1, 6.

5. What must you do in order to gain charity? Moroni 7:48.

6. What are the qualities of charity you should have in your lives? Moroni 7:45.

7. Charity is learning to love as Christ loved; loving God and loving Christ are exemplified in our loving our fellowman. How will the Lord know that you are his disciple? John 13:34–35.

8. What are the fruits of having the love of God in your hearts? 4 Nephi 1:15–16.

9. How can you show your love? John 14:15.

10. Those who love God are given the _____. Doctrine and Covenants 76:116.

11. What can the Holy Ghost fill you with? Moroni 8:26.

Truly, all the law and the prophets hang on love of God and your fellowmen. (See Matthew 22:36–40.) Love is the great commandment. Love is the motive for all of Heavenly Father's and the Savior's actions. Love should be the motive for all of your actions. The joy of loving is the joy of life. With love, life will become sweet. You will be happy, and then on your mission the new converts will say, when asked why they joined, "I felt the missionaries' love so much I had to listen to what they said. While listening, I felt the Spirit and knew I had to be baptized. I had to come unto Christ." And it all began with love.

THINGS TO DO

1. Visit the sick, the elderly, and the homeless, and plan to serve them with food, loving conversations, and gospel instruction.

2. Pray for charity so that you may be able to bless others.

3. Write a letter of love and support to a friend.

4. Start a good conversation, and share the gospel with an acquaintance.

5. Show your love by caring and serving your fellowman. Do something to aid them.

6. Read the following statements by the prophets. Then underline or highlight important points.

Ezra Taft Benson: You will not be an effective missionary until you learn to have sympathy for all of our Father's children—unless you learn to love them. People can feel when love is extended to them. Many yearn for it. When you sympathize with their feelings, they in turn will reciprocate goodwill to you. You will have made a friend. And as the Prophet Joseph Smith taught, "Whom can I preach to but my friends." Yes, love the people.
    —*Teachings of Ezra Taft Benson,* p. 206.

Joseph Smith: A man filled with the love of God, is not content with blessing his family alone, but ranges through the whole world, anxious to bless the whole human race.
    —*History of the Church,* 4:227.

Marvin J. Ashton: We must at regular and appropriate intervals speak and reassure others of our love and the long time it takes to prove it by our actions. Real love does take time. The Great Shepherd had the same thoughts in mind when he taught, "If ye love me, *keep* my commandments" (John 14:15; italics added) and "If ye love me *feed* my sheep" (John 21:16; italics added). Love demands action if it is to be continuing. Love is a process. Love is not a declaration. Love is not an announcement. Love is not a passing fancy. Love is not an expediency. Love is not a convenience. "If ye love me, keep my commandments" and "If ye love me feed my sheep" are God-given proclamations that should remind us we can often best show our love through the processes of *feeding* and *keeping.* . . .

The opportunities for showing love for God through the home, neighborhood, mission field, community, and family are never-ending. Some of us are inclined to terminate our love processes in the family when a member disappoints, rebels, or becomes lost. Sometimes when family members least deserve love, they need it the most. Love is not appropriately expressed in threats, accusations, expressions of disappointment, or retaliation. Real love takes time, patience, help, and continuing performances.
    —*Conference Report,* October 1975, pp. 160, 163.

James E. Faust: Because of his rebellion, Lucifer was cast out and became Satan, the devil, "the father of all lies, to deceive and to blind men, and to lead them captive at his will, even as many as would not hearken unto [his] voice." (Moses 4:4.) . . . Does this not place some responsibility on the followers of Christ to show concern for loved ones who have lost their way and "are shut out from the presence of God"? (Moses 6:49.) I know of no better way to do this than to show unconditional love and to help lost souls seek another path.
    —*Reach Up for the Light* (Salt Lake City: Deseret Book Company, 1990), p. 105.

CHAPTER 9

OBEDIENCE

Learning to obey before and during your mission will bring you the blessings of heaven in all things, especially the guidance and blessings of the Spirit. Through obedience, you gain self-mastery and self-discipline. Being obedient reflects the amount of love you possess for the Savior.

1. To _____ is better than to sacrifice. 1. Samuel 15:22.

2. What does Doctrine and Covenants 130:20–21 teach you in regard to obedience?

3. The great law and doctrine of the Atonement were brought forth by the grace and love of God and Jesus Christ. Because Christ came to do the will of the Father, he worked out his magnificent atonement. He was obedient. What must you do to be saved? Doctrine and Covenants 138:4.

4. The Sons of Helaman were not just obedient; they obeyed with _____. Alma 57:21.

5. The third line of the third stanza of "Our Savior's Love" reads, "I love his law; I will obey." Why do you obey and keep the commandments of God? John 14:15.

6. You are free to choose. You are truly free when you covenant to obey God because the chains of sin that bind you are thereby broken. What are some of the blessings of keeping the commandments?

Mosiah 5:9.

Mosiah 2:41.

1 John 2:5.

Moroni 4.

7. What happens when we disobey and fail to keep the commandments?
Mormon 1:13–14.

Doctrine and Covenants 56:3.

Doctrine and Covenants 59:21.

8. How does the Lord help you keep the commandments? 1 Nephi 3:7.

9. What is our real test here on earth? Abraham 3:25.

As you learn to obey, you receive blessings from your Heavenly Father—happiness here and in the hereafter. (See Mosiah 2:41.) You enjoy the gifts of the Spirit. Your self-respect increases. You become self-disciplined and gain self-mastery. All these are important to missionary success. Obedience leads to a shower of the blessings of heaven. That's why obedience is the first law of heaven. Adam exemplified this with these immortal words: "I know not, save the Lord commanded me." (Moses 5:6.) You should have this kind of faithful obedience. As you grow in the love of God and of Jesus Christ, you will keep their commandments.

THINGS TO DO

1. These two exercises will help you learn to obey with exactness: (a) Get up early at a specified time. (b) Study the scriptures early in the morning and again in the evening each day.

2. Set several goals and make plans to achieve them.

3. Make a list of commandments you need to live better, and obey them with exactness.

4. Read the following statements by the prophets. Then underline or highlight important points.

Joseph Smith: To get salvation we must not only do some things, but everything which God has commanded. Men may preach and practice everything except those things which God commands us to do, and will be damned at last. We may tithe mint and rue, and all manner of herbs, and still not obey the commandments of God. The object with me is to obey and teach others to obey God in just what He tells us to do. It mattereth not whether the principle is popular or unpopular, I will always maintain a true principle, even if I stand alone in it.
—*History of the Church,* 6:223.

Joseph F. Smith: The important consideration is not how long we can live but how well we can learn the lessons of life, and discharge our duties and obligations to God and to each other. One of the main purposes of our existence is that we might conform to the image and likeness of Him who sojourned in the flesh without blemish—immaculate, pure and spotless! Christ came not only to atone for the sins of the world, but to set an example before all men and to establish the standard of God's perfection, of God's law, and of obedience to the Father. . . .

To please [God] we must not only worship him with thanksgiving and praise but render willing obedience to his commandments. By so doing he is bound to bestow his blessings; for it is upon this principle (obedience to law) that all blessings are predicated.
—As quoted by F. W. Otterstrom, in "A Journey to the South: Gems from President Smith's Talks to the People on the Way," *Improvement Era,* December 1917, p. 104.

Mark E. Petersen: There is only one cure for the evils of this world, and for the broken hearts of men and women, and that is faith in the Lord Jesus Christ, and the living of that faith by obedience to the commandments of the Lord our God. There is nothing that can compare with it. There is no other answer. It is obedience to Christ, or it is dissolution.
—Conference Report, October 1963, p. 122.

Spencer W. Kimball: When men obey commands of a creator, it is not blind obedience. How different is the cowering of a subject to his totalitarian monarch and the dignified, willing obedience one gives to his God. The dictator is ambitious, selfish, and has ulterior motives. God's every command is righteous, every directive purposeful, and all for the good of the governed. The first may be blind obedience, but the latter is certainly faith obedience.

—Conference Report, October 1954, p. 52.

Joseph F. Smith: We believe that God's will is to exalt men; that the liberty that comes through obedience to the Gospel of Jesus Christ is the greatest measure of liberty that can come to man.

—Conference Report, April 1904, p. 4.

Boyd K. Packer: Some who do not understand the doctrinal part do not readily see the relationship between obedience and agency. And they miss one vital connection and see obedience only as restraint. They then resist the very thing that will give them true freedom. There is no true freedom without responsibility, and there is no enduring freedom without a knowledge of the truth. . . . We are the sons and daughters of God, willing followers, disciples of the Lord Jesus Christ, and "under this head are [we] made free." (Mosiah 5:8.)

—Conference Report, April 1983, p. 89.

SECTION 3

PERSONAL PREPARATION

CONVERSION AND TESTIMONY

QUALIFYING FOR THE WORK

CREATE, PLAN, AND ORGANIZE
FOR SUCCESS AND HAPPINESS

KNOWLEDGE

THE BOOK OF MORMON AND YOU

DILIGENCE WITH FAITH IN THE
STRENGTH OF THE LORD

CHAPTER 10

CONVERSION AND TESTIMONY

To become an instrument in the hands of the Lord, you should truly come unto Christ. This requires conversion of your heart and soul to the gospel and church of Jesus Christ. Then with faith and by the power of the Spirit, you can bear witness of all the gospel truths.

1. In the process of conversion, many principles are involved in bringing about the mighty change of heart, or being born of God. The following scriptures identify different things you should know, feel, or do in becoming converted. List them below:

Joel 2:12.

Mosiah 3:19.

Acts 3:19.

Alma 5:12–15.

Mosiah 5:7.

Mosiah 27:25.

Alma 38:6.

Mosiah 18:8–9.

Doctrine and Covenants 20:37.

Luke 22:32.

2. Conversion occurs on the inside — in the heart; your inner nature is changed through the Lord Jesus Christ.
What will be your desires? Helaman 10:5.

What is your will? John 5:30.

What will be your work? Moses 1:39.

Where will be your thought and affections? Alma 37:36.

3. You become converted by the Spirit through the power of the word. You change, just as Alma 31:5 shows. With prayer, study, and righteousness, your testimony grows. The blessing of bearing it can help others come unto Christ. The following scriptures teach us great principles and blessings concerning testimony. List them from each scripture.
1 Corinthians 1:5–6.

1 Corinthians 12:3.

2 Timothy 1:8.

Alma 4:19.

Alma 30:40–41.

Helaman 9:39.

Ether 12:6.

Doctrine and Covenants 6:31.

Doctrine and Covenants 58:6–7.

Doctrine and Covenants 62:3.

As you live a Christlike life, you bear witness of your conversion and testimony. You desire to bless others. You want to be a Saint—a gospel-oriented Saint through the atonement of Jesus Christ. You will be a light and a savior to mankind, for you will hold up the light, even the Lord Jesus Christ. You will become a mighty instrument in the hands of the Lord.

THINGS TO DO

1. Consider Mosiah 18:8–9. Write down one thing you can do to fill the covenant described in the verses, then implement it.

2. Prepare a pure testimony of your beliefs and bear it on Fast Sunday.

3. Read the following statements by the prophets. Then underline or highlight important points.

Ezra Taft Benson: You must have a burning testimony of the divinity of this work if you are going to succeed. Now it is almost a foregone conclusion that missionaries, when they come into the field, have that testimony. Sometimes there will be missionaries who are not quite certain. Then your first obligation is to get that testimony through prayer, through fasting, through meditation, through study, through appealing to the Lord to give you the testimony, through responding to calls when they come to you. You must have a testimony of the divinity of this work. You must know that God lives; that Jesus is the Christ, the Redeemer of the world; that Joseph Smith is a prophet of God; that the priesthood and authority of our Heavenly Father is here; and that you bear that priesthood and have the authority to represent him in the world.
   —*God, Family, Country,* pp. 60–61.

Spencer W. Kimball: Every man should give to the people his testimony. Every one of you, every one of you should be a missionary in addition to what else you are doing. You have neighbors, you have friends, you have fellow workers; it's your responsibility. You cannot go into eternity and look the Lord in the face if you've done nothing toward teaching the gospel to others. Have your wives do the same.
   —*Sao Paulo Area Conference Report,* 1975, p. 52.

Joseph Fielding Smith: Every missionary who goes out should see to it that he leaves his testimony, so that he will be free as the Lord has declared he should be in section four of the Doctrine and Covenants; and so that every man with whom he comes in contact should be warned and left without excuse, and thus the blood of every man may be upon his own head.
   —*Conference Report,* April 1946, p. 158.

Thomas S. Monson: Our missionaries are not salesmen with wares to peddle; rather, they are servants of the Most High God, with testimonies to bear, truths to teach, and souls to save.
   —*Conference Report,* October 1987, p. 52.

Ezra Taft Benson: A most priceless blessing available to every member of the Church is a testimony of the divinity of Jesus Christ and His church. A testimony is one of the few possessions we may take with us when we leave this life.
   To have a testimony of Jesus is to possess knowledge through the Holy Ghost of the divine mission of Jesus Christ.
   A testimony of Jesus is to know the divine nature of our Lord's birth—that He is indeed the *Only* Begotten Son in the flesh. . . .
   To possess a testimony of Jesus is to know that He voluntarily took upon Himself

the sins of all mankind in the Garden of Gethsemane, which caused Him to suffer in both body and spirit and to bleed from every pore. All this He did so that we would not have to suffer if we would repent. (See D&C 19:16, 18.)

To possess a testimony of Jesus is to know that He came forth triumphantly from the grave with a physical, resurrected body. And because He lives, so shall all mankind.

To possess a testimony of Jesus is to know that God the Father and Jesus Christ did indeed appear to the Prophet Joseph Smith to establish a new dispensation of His gospel so that salvation may be preached to all nations before He comes.

To possess a testimony of Jesus is to know that the Church, which He established in the meridian of time and restored in modern times is, as the Lord has declared, "the only true and living church upon the face of the whole earth." (D&C 1:30.)

Having such a testimony is vital. But of even greater importance is being valiant in our testimony.

A testimony of Jesus means that we accept the divine mission of Jesus Christ, embrace His gospel, and do His works. It also means we accept the prophetic mission of Joseph Smith and his successors and follow their counsel. As Jesus said, "Whether by mine own voice or by the voice of my servants, it is the same." (D&C 1:38.)

—"Valiant in the Testimony of Jesus," *Ensign,* February 1987, p. 2.

CHAPTER 11

QUALIFYING FOR THE WORK

To volunteer to serve the Lord is good. To become a qualified ambassador of Christ is wonderful. The latter requires a willingness to become a worthy instrument through sanctification and hard work.

1. How do you serve God? Doctrine and Covenants 4:2.

2. Record the definitions of *heart, might, mind* and *strength.* (If possible, use a large Bible dictionary for *heart.*)

3. The answers to numbers one and two above teach you how you should work as you serve the Lord. Write in your own words what this means to you.

4. What is the blessing of serving with all your heart, might, mind, and strength? Doctrine and Covenants 4:2.

5. When people recognize and remember the covenants, tender mercies, and goodness of God, their love of God will increase to the point of total dependence, in righteousness, on God. Thus they become humble, like the poor Zoramites who were prepared to hear the word (see Alma 32:6) so they could be taught to understand the atonement of Christ and his life-saving gospel. When you understand and

appreciate these things, you become grateful, which is the beginning of all *righteous desire*. This desire brings about the best reason to serve in pure righteousness. Work for this desire, and then _____ (D&C 4:3). What glory and joy there are in representing the Savior Jesus Christ.

6. What is the reward for whoever "thrusteth in his sickle with his might"? Doctrine and Covenants 4:4.

7. In Doctrine and Covenants 4:5–6, many attributes are listed that will qualify you for the work. This in an ongoing process that will help you become Christlike, obtaining the power to bring souls to Christ in love. Define the following and give an example of each. (Use the LDS Bible Dictionary before using a regular dictionary)
Faith:

Hope:

Charity (love):

An eye single to the glory of God:

Virtue:

Knowledge:

Temperance:

Patience:

Brotherly kindness:

Godliness:

Humility:

Diligence:

8. What great principle is taught in Doctrine and Covenants 4:7, and how should we practice it?

Preparing and qualifying for the work are exciting processes. Remember, preparation precedes power: if you are prepared, you will not fear. (See D&C 38:30.) The Lord will bless you as you treasure things up in your heart. (See D&C 84:85.) You will be like Nephi when you give yourself to the Lord. The Lord will prepare a way for you (see 1 Nephi 3:7) to qualify for the work. Remember, the Lord gives you weaknesses so you can become humble, and if you are humble, he will make you strong (see Ether 12:27), just as Ammon experienced (see Alma 26:12). In strength of the Lord, you can do all things.

THINGS TO DO

1. Go to your topical guide and list some of the scriptures under each topic from number seven above. You could make a booklet with these topics, as well as a plan to acquire these attributes as you prepare to serve the Lord.

2. Commit Doctrine and Covenants 4 to memory, and repeat it daily to remind you to prepare for the work.

3. Read the following statements by the prophets. Then underline or highlight important points.

Brigham Young: If the Elders cannot go with clean hands and pure hearts, they had better stay here. Do not go thinking, when you arrive at the Missouri River, at the Mississippi, at the Ohio, or at the Atlantic, that then you will purify yourselves; but start from here with clean hands and pure hearts, and be pure from the crown of the head to the soles of your feet; then live so every hour. Go in that manner, and in that manner labor, and return again as clean as a piece of pure white paper. This is the way to go; and if you do not do that, your hearts will ache.

—*Discourses of Brigham Young*, p. 323.

Spencer W. Kimball: Humility is essential in missionary work. To convince people of the divinity of the work one must of necessity be humble. To be arrogant or "cocky" is to threaten to drive away the Holy Ghost who alone can convince and bring testimonies.

—*Teachings of Spencer W. Kimball*, p. 569.

Wilford Woodruff: All the messengers in the vineyard should be righteous and holy men and call upon the Lord in mighty prayer, in order to prevail. It is the privilege of every Elder in Israel, who is laboring in the vineyard, if he will live up to his privileges, to have dreams, visions and revelations, and the Holy Ghost as a constant companion, that he may be able thoroughly to gather out the blood of Israel and the meek of the earth, and bring them into the fold of Christ.

—"An Epistle from the President of the Twelve Apostles," *Millennial Star*, 20 December 1886, p. 805.

Ezra Taft Benson: A two-year mission today requires good physical health. It requires that you keep your body clean. In your early teenage years, when temptations come to you to take things into your body which are unsuitable, have the courage to resist. Live the Word of Wisdom—no smoking, no drinking of any alcoholic beverages, and no drugs. Keep your body pure—a pure vessel for the Lord.

Stay morally clean. This means that you keep a clean mind. Your thoughts will determine you actions, and so they must be controlled. It's difficult to control those thoughts if you submit yourself to temptation. So you will have to carefully select your reading material, the movies you see, and the other forms of entertainment in order to have good thoughts rather than unwholesome desires.

—*Ensign*, May 1985, p. 36.

John Taylor: The kind of men we want as bearers of this Gospel message are men who have faith in God; men who have faith in their religion; men who honor their Priesthood; men in whom the people who know them have faith and in whom God has confidence, and not some poor unfortunate beings who are wanted to leave a place because they cannot live in it; but we want men full of the Holy Ghost and the power of God that they may go forth weeping, bearing precious seed and sowing the seeds of eternal life, and then returning with gladness, bringing their sheaves with them. . . . Men who bear the words of life among the nations, ought to be men of honor, integrity, virtue and purity; and this being the command of God to us, we shall try and carry it out.

—*Journal of Discourses*, 21:375.

Heber J. Grant: There is nothing that qualifies a man so much for preaching the gospel of the Lord Jesus Christ as to study the revelations that the Lord has seen fit to give us in our day.

—*Conference Report*, October 1925, p. 6.

CHAPTER 12

CREATE, PLAN, AND ORGANIZE FOR SUCCESS AND HAPPINESS

Organizing and planning your life will bring direction, security, and peace of mind. Preparing well for your mission will reduce the anxiety you sometimes feel and bring the Spirit into your life.

1. List the things you can do to better prepare, as described in Doctrine and Covenants 88:118–19.

2. Who will show you all things that you should do? 2 Nephi 32:5.

3. Make a list of some things the Spirit could show you to do (i.e., to pray, to study, to learn).

4. Planning is a key to success. It involves the "creation of" or the "organization of" many things. What did God organize? Abraham 4:1, 27.

What did God create? Refer to the following scriptures.
Moses 2:27.

Moses 3:5, 7.

Moses 7:64.

5. From question number four you can see that Heavenly Father and his Son plan and organize to bless your life. What should your plans for your life reflect?

6. List the items described in Doctrine and Covenants 88:74 that help in preparing "every needful thing" (D&C 88:119).

7. Read Doctrine and Covenants 88:75–80. Notice all the things the Lord will do and we should do in order to be better prepared. What is the purpose of all of this preparation, as described in Doctrine and Covenants 88:74–80?

The key is to prepare every needful thing. Being spiritually in tune is difficult unless you are carefully and properly organized. If you are always disorganized, you feel out of control and overwhelmed. Organizing your priorities according to your responsibilities in life as well as your missionary service will make you more productive and bring you the joy of peace.

THINGS TO DO

1. If you have not already done so, set a deadline to complete this workbook. Establish a plan to work through a certain number of pages each day.

2. Make a list of the scriptures you wish to read, feasting upon (see 2 Nephi 32:3), and living by every word (see D&C 84:43–45), and make a plan to search them at a regular time or to read a certain number of pages each day. The resolution may be as simple as reading the Book of Mormon through.

3. Take your list of attributes from Doctrine and Covenants 4 and establish a plan to improve on each one. Be sure to include deadlines for your plan of action.

4. Pray and plan to visualize bringing souls to Christ and enjoying the Lord's success. Read Alma 17:4; 29:13–14; Ether 12:14.

5. Make a list of every needful thing—that is, everything you need to do financially, physically, mentally, socially, emotionally, and spiritually. It might include books, money, clothes, passport, things to complete prior to departure, or letters of love and appreciation to those who have helped you. Devise a timetable to complete them.

6. Write a statement of what kind of missionary you are going to be and read it every day (now and throughout your mission).

7. Make a schedule to follow for a week that will help you "discipline" yourself as well as assist you in accomplishing your goals.

8. Make a missionary book full of scriptures, talks, stories, poems, and ideas for your mission. Set a deadline to complete it.

9. Read the following statements by the prophets. Then underline or highlight important points.

Ezra Taft Benson: The missionary is entitled to inspiration in choosing his personal goals; and when he has sought the Lord through prayer and meditation, he will be motivated best by those goals he selects himself and commits himself to attain.
    —*Teachings of Ezra Taft Benson,* p. 200.

Spencer W. Kimball: Time should be used efficiently. In the matter of compensation, how would you like it if the Lord changed his policy, and instead of the compensation already promised he would substitute dollars? Suppose he now said, "Missionary, from today on I pay you $5 an hour for your services, but for only those sacred hours of actual proselyting. And there will be a special bonus of $1,000 for each person whom you baptize who is thoroughly converted." Analyze your own reactions. Would you change your work habits? Would the fringe demands on your time increase or decrease? Would letter writing, toilet making, study, recreation, travel, be reduced? Would the day be planned more methodically and efficiently? Would the Saturdays and Sundays be clean-up days, and for what would holidays be used? Would you reorganize your day?
    —*Teachings of Spencer W. Kimball,* p. 576.

Spencer W. Kimball: Such planning must begin early, it has been said that "even the very longest journey begins with a single first step." So when that first step is made it must be on a properly charted course. Otherwise, habits come upon us unawares, and sin has us in its clutches before we realize it.

As well as establishing worthy goals, charting the course prevents one from living an unplanned, haphazard life—a tumbleweed existence. . . .

Smart young people will discipline themselves early in youth, charting long-range courses to include all that is wholesome and nothing that is ruinous. The bridge builder, before starting construction, draws charts and plans, makes estimates of strains and stresses, costs and hazards; the architect, even before excavation, makes a blueprint of the building from foundation to pinnacle. Similarly the smart person will plan carefully and blueprint his own life from his first mental awakening to the end of life. "Just as a builder will wish his structure to stand through storm and disturbances of the elements, so the young and old alike will wish a life unharmed by adversities, calamities, and troubles throughout eternity. Having planned such a course, prudent men will gear their lives, activities, ambitions and aspirations so that they may have every advantage in total fulfillment of a righteous destiny."

—*Miracle of Forgiveness,* pp. 233–35.

CHAPTER 13

KNOWLEDGE

You are the messengers of the *message*. You are called to preach his word that mankind might come unto Christ and be perfected in him. As a missionary, you need the knowledge of the plan of salvation, as well as a knowledge of what and how to teach, in order to preach the gospel of Jesus Christ.

1. The Lord taught Hyrum Smith two important things that apply to you in regard to teaching his word. What are they? Doctrine and Covenants 11:21–22.

2. What did the sons of Mosiah do in order to be "men of a sound understanding" and wax "strong in the knowledge of the truth"? Alma 17:2.

3. The priests described in Mosiah 18:26 taught with the power and authority of God. What two things did they have that helped them do this?

4. What gave Ammon the knowledge to teach? Alma 18:35.

5. What are some ways you can gain knowledge, as mentioned in Doctrine and Covenants 109:7?

6. What is required of you in order to gain knowledge? Doctrine and Covenants 1:28.

7. How did Oliver Cowdery receive knowledge? Doctrine and Covenants 8:1–3.

8. If you ask, you shall receive _____ upon _____ and _____ upon _____. Doctrine and Covenants 42:61.

9. What is the wonderful gift of the Spirit mentioned in Doctrine and Covenants 46:18?

10. The pure knowledge as described in Doctrine and Covenants 121:42 shall greatly _____.

Some of the scriptures you have just read relate knowledge to power. The knowledge of God and his son is life eternal. (See John 17:3.) When you understand the doctrines and principles of the gospel and kingdom of God, you gain an appreciation of truth. With knowledge, your desire to share the restored gospel will bear fruit. Many converts say, when asked, "Why did you change?" They often answer, "The missionaries had the answers to my questions." Prepare to know the things of God, and then present it in mildness and meekness by the Spirit.

Nephi said, "I did read many things unto them which were written in the books of Moses; but that I might more fully persuade them to believe in the Lord their Redeemer I did read unto them that which was written by the prophet Isaiah; *for I did liken all scriptures unto us, that it might be for our profit and learning.*" (1 Nephi 19:23; italics added.)

All scriptures are for your profit and learning. Take all of them personally, applying them to your life. The word of God is for you to live today. The fullness of the gospel is in your life as you live the word of God.

A WAY TO APPLY THE SCRIPTURES TO YOUR LIFE

1. Read the scriptural passage carefully.

2. Ponder on how it relates to you.

3. Record the scriptural reference (chapter and verse) and the main idea as it apples to you.

4. Write a personal statement as to how you are going to live the scripture.

Here are some examples (for some scriptures, you can write more than one application):

1 Nephi 3:7   I will keep the commandments because the Lord will help me by preparing the way. Special assignment: I will love my companion by doing a kind deed, writing a note of appreciation, or offering a prayer in his/her behalf.

1 Nephi 4:6	I will be believing and faithful, because if I'm righteous in my desire, the Spirit will lead me.
Alma 26:27	I will realize my own weaknesses and refrain from boasting. I will rely on the strength of the Lord.
Doctrine and Covenants 60: 2–3	I will open my mouth to find, teach, challenge, and commit my investigators.
Doctrine and Covenants 95: 1–2	Because the Lord loves me, he will "chastise" me. I can repent faster and better because of the guilt I feel over my sins. The chastisement for my sins is to deliver me from temptation.
James 1:22–25	I will turn hearing to action. Rather than forget, I will work and show my level of faith.
Matthew 22: 36–40	I will show my love for God and my neighbors through service and obedience. I will make the development of love my number one priority because everything else hangs on it.
Alma 29:9–10	I glory in being an instrument in the hands of the Lord. I will prepare every needful thing to be a better instrument for the Lord.

Following is a list of scriptures from the Doctrine and Covenants. They will help you prepare now, as well as in the field. Feast upon them; apply them to your life. In a notebook, record how you intend to apply them to your life. (See 1 Nephi 19:23.) Indeed, the power of the word can help change lives more than anything else on this earth.

1:4–5	Missionaries go forth with the voice of warning.
1:18–19	Proclaim the word; weak things will overcome the strong; trust not in the arm of the flesh.
1:23–24	Fullness of the gospel proclaimed by the weak and simple; these commandments given by God for the understanding of his servants.
1:38	All shall be fulfilled by the voice of Christ or his servants—it is the same.
4:2–3	Serve with your heart, might, mind, and strength, and then you can stand blameless; with a desire to serve God, you are called.
4:4–5	He that thrusts in his sickle brings salvation to his soul; certain attributes and an eye single to God qualify him for the work.
4:6–7	Certain principles and attributes of character qualify one to ask and receive.
5:16	Whoever believes on God's words will be visited by the manifestation of his spirit.
6:3	He that thrusts in a sickle and reaps will treasure up salvation for his soul.
6:14–15	Ask and be enlightened by the Spirit of truth.

6:22–23	Ask and have peace spoken to your mind; what greater witness than that from God (through the Spirit)?
7:4–5	John the Beloved desired to bring souls to Christ, to do more among the living—a greater work than what he had done.
8:2–5	The spirit of revelation is being told in your heart and mind by the Spirit; it is Oliver Cowdery's gift of protection.
8:10	Without faith, you can do nothing; do not ask for what you should not.
9:5–9	Continue what you have begun; don't murmur; asking is not enough if we take no thought; burning of the bosom is one way to receive an answer.
10:63	Establish the gospel that there may be no contention.
24:12	Oliver Cowdery to open his mouth to declare the gospel; he shall receive strength.
24:19	Prune the vineyard for the last time.
27:15–18	Take upon you the armor of Christ.
28:8	Oliver Cowdery to preach to the Lamanites.
29:4–7	Chosen to declare the word; Christ is in your midst; pray and ask in faith; gather the elect.
30:1–3	David Whitmer's problem with the fear of man; his mind on things of the earth, not on God.
30:5–6	Peter Whitmer to open his mouth and preach; will be afflicted.
31:3–13	Rejoice in your mission; declare the word; thrust in your sickle; your sins are forgiven, and you'll be laden with sheaves; people's hearts will be opened; you can strengthen them; be patient; be a physician to the church; Comforter to guide you; pray always; be faithful.
32:1	Parley P. Pratt to declare the gospel, learn of Jesus, and be meek and lowly.
32:3	Preach and Christ will be in midst for protection.
32:4	Give heed to the written word and pretend to no other revelation.
33:2	Lift up your voice as with the sound of a trump.
33:3–4	Last time laborers are called to the vineyard; it is corrupt.
33:8–11	Open your mouth; you will be laden with sheaves; preach repentance and baptism.
33:16	Scriptures given for your instruction; Spirit quickeneth all things.
33:17	Be prepared with your lamps for the coming of the Bridegroom.
34:5–6	Blessed because you are called to preach and prepare way for Second Coming.
34:10	Spare not from preaching by the power of the Holy Ghost.

35:13–14	Unlearned called to thrash the nations by the power of God's spirit; their arms will be Christ's arms; he will be their shield and buckler.
35:15	The poor and the meek shall hear the gospel.
36:6–7	Cry repentance; every man who embraces the gospel may be ordained and sent forth.
50:13–25	Called to preach the gospel; preach no other way but by the Spirit; receive the word of truth by the Spirit; such a person is edified (given light).
50:26–30	Whoever is ordained of God is appointed to be greatest; a possessor of all things if purified and cleansed from all sin. When you ask in the name of Jesus, it shall be done; if you are appointed the head, the spirits shall be subject to you.
52:9	Preach what prophets have written and what the Comforter teaches through the prayer of faith.
52:21–27	Calling of several missionaries to preach by the way.
52:33	Every missionary to proselyte in an appointed area and not in someone else's area.
52:40	Remember the poor and the needy, the sick and afflicted.
53:3	Commission of an elder to preach faith, repentance, remission of sins, and reception of the Holy Ghost.
58:6	You are sent that you might be obedient and bear testimony.
58:47	Preach in all places to all kinds of people.
58:59, 63	Missionary to bear record of what he believes and knows and of what has been revealed to him.
60:13	Don't idle away your time or bury your talents.
60:14	Proclaim the word, but not in haste, wrath, or strife.
61:33–34	Declare the word, and you shall rid your garments so that they shall be spotless.
62:5	Bear record two by two; be faithful and declare glad tidings.
64:8–9	Disciples of old were afflicted and chastened for contention and lack of forgiveness; modern-day disciples should not seek occasion against each other.
66:5–8	Proclaim the gospel where it has not been proclaimed; bear testimony in every place; train your new companion.
67:3	Elders don't receive blessings because of fear in their hearts.
67:10	To see and know God, you must strip yourselves of jealousy and fears and be humble.
88:84	Labor diligently so you may be perfected in your ministry.
88:118–127	Seek wisdom; establish a house of God; cease from wickedness; teach in order; proper sleep habits commanded; have charity; pray always; school of the prophets (compare to MTC) established for instruction.

88:137	School of the prophets (compare to MTC) to be a tabernacle of the Holy Spirit to your edification.
90:11	Everyone to hear the fullness of the gospel in his or her own tongue.
93:39	Light of truth taken away because of disobedience and traditions of our fathers.
93:46	Missionaries are servants for the world's and the Lord's sake.
95:1–2	Lord chastens those whom he loves; chastisement prepares a way for deliverance from sin.
95:10	In training (the school of the prophets), contention arose, and they had to be chastened.
97:3–5	School in Zion (compare to MTC) established; Parley P. Pratt to be teacher and blessed to expound all scriptures and mysteries.
97:6	Lord will show mercy, but some need to be chastened.
97:13–14	A house of thanksgiving and instruction (compare to MTC) to be built so saints may be perfected.
98:12–13	Learn line upon line (continual steadfastness), and you will be proved; whoever lays down his life for the cause shall have eternal life.
99:1–3	John Murdock to proclaim the gospel from house to house despite persecution; whoever receives him receives Lord; he will be able to declare the word through the Holy Spirit.
100:1–8	Lord will take care of families; doors will be opened so souls can have salvation; the Lord will put in your heart the thoughts you should speak; declare it in the name of Christ with solemnity and meekness; the Holy Ghost shall bear record.
101:35–40	Those who suffer for the Lord in their call will receive glory; care not for the body but for the soul; you are the salt of the earth, but if the salt lose its savor, it is "good for nothing."
101:60–62	Commanded to be faithful and wise steward.
103:9–10	*Missionaries* are lights to the world and to be saviors of men; if not, they are as salt without savor.
103:27–28	Whoever lays his life down for the Lord will find it; Christ's disciples are willing to do so.
104:11–13	Just as in the United Order, all men and women are accountable for their stewardships.

THINGS TO DO

1. Purchase a copy of the *Missionary Gospel Study Guide*. Make a plan to complete reading it and the associated material, if possible, prior to entering the Missionary Training Center. It will greatly bless your life.

2. Become familiar with the standard missionary discussions by reading and attempting to explain each principle in the discussions.

3. Accompany the full-time missionaries—you will see that you can do it too.

4. Read the following statements by the prophets. Then underline or highlight important points.

Joseph F. Smith: We may know all about the philosophy of the ages and the history of the nations of the earth; we may study the wisdom and knowledge of man and get all the information that we can acquire in a lifetime of research and study, but all of it put together will never qualify any one to become a minister of the Gospel unless he has the knowledge and spirit of the first principles of the Gospel of Jesus Christ.
    —Conference Report, April 1915, p. 138.

Ezra Taft Benson: Anyone who has diligently sought to know the doctrines and teachings of the Book of Mormon and has used it conscientiously in missionary work knows within his soul that this is the instrument which God has given to the missionaries to convince the Jew and Gentile and Lamanite of the truthfulness of our message.
    —*Teachings of Ezra Taft Benson,* p. 204.

George Albert Smith: It is not sufficient that a young man or woman signify his desire, because of his confidence in his parents, to do what they would have him do, go into the world and preach the gospel; it is not sufficient that they answer the call that our Heavenly Father makes from time to time through his servants for mission service; but it is also necessary that they qualify for the work, search the scriptures, and learn what the Lord would have them know. It is important that our sons and daughters become established in their faith and know as their parents know that this is our Father's work.
    —*Sharing the Gospel with Others,* compiled Preston Nibley (Salt Lake City: Deseret Book Company, 1948), p. 13.

Ezra Taft Benson: As missionaries, you must learn to love the scriptures. Your purpose for being in the mission field is to save souls, to baptize converts, to bring converted families into the Lord's Church. I ask you to give particular attention to scriptures which explain your holy calling, such as Doctrine and Covenants sections 4, 11, 15, 16, and 18, and the Book of Mormon.
    —*Teachings of Ezra Taft Benson,* p. 204.

Joseph Smith: Add to your faith knowledge, etc. The principle of knowledge is the principle of salvation. This principle can be comprehended by the faithful and diligent; and every one that does not obtain knowledge sufficient to be saved will be condemned. The principle of salvation is given us through the knowledge of Jesus Christ.
    —*Teachings of the Prophet Joseph Smith,* p. 297.

David O. McKay: Eternal life is the result of knowledge, and knowledge is obtained by doing the will of God.
    —*Gospel Ideals* (Salt Lake City: Improvement Era, 1953), p. 8.

Brigham Young, Heber C. Kimball, Willard Richards (First Presidency): If men would be great in goodness, they must be intelligent, for no man can do good unless he knows how; therefore seek after knowledge, all knowledge, and especially that which is from above, which is wisdom to direct in all things, and if you find any thing that God does not know, you need not learn that thing; but strive to know what God knows, and use that knowledge as God uses it, and then you will be like him; will see as you are seen, and know as you are known; and have charity, love one another, and do each other good continually, and forever, even as for yourselves.

—*Messages of the First Presidency, 1833–1964,* compiled James R. Clark (Salt Lake City: Bookcraft, 1965), p. 86.

Joseph Smith: Knowledge through our Lord and Savior Jesus Christ is the grand key that unlocks the glories and mysteries of the kingdom of heaven.

—*History of the Church,* 5:389.

THE BOOK OF MORMON AND YOU

In 1829, the Lord warned the Saints that they were to "trifle not with sacred things." (D&C 6:12.) Surely the Book of Mormon is a sacred thing, yet many trifle with it, or in other words, take it lightly, treating it as though it were of little importance. In 1832, as some early missionaries returned from their fields of labor, the Lord reproved them for treating the Book of Mormon lightly. He said that as a result of their attitude, their minds had been darkened. Not only had treating this sacred book lightly brought a loss of light to them, it had also brought the whole church under condemnation, even all the children of Zion. And then the Lord said, "They shall remain under this condemnation until they repent and remember the new covenant, even the Book of Mormon." (D&C 84:54–57.)

Reading, studying, feasting, searching, and living the word of God from the Book of Mormon are musts for all Saints, but more especially for the Lord's missionaries.

1. What is the promise? If you read the Book of Mormon and ask _____ with a sincere _____, with _____, having _____, God will manifest the truth of it unto you, _____. Moroni 10:4.

2. How do you get to the tree of life? 1 Nephi 15:23–24; Alma 32:40–43.

3. The Book of Mormon is the word of God. From the following Book of Mormon scriptures, list all the blessings and cautions the word of God can give you as it applies to your life.

   1 Nephi 17:31.

   2 Nephi 27:14.

2 Nephi 32:3.

Jacob 4:9; Mormon 9:17.

Omni 1:13.

Mosiah 1:4–7.

Mosiah 26:3.

Alma 4:19.

Alma 5:7.

Alma 12:10.

Alma 17:2.

Alma 31:5.

Alma 34:6.

Alma 37:44.

Alma 44:5.

Helaman 3:29–30.

4 Nephi 1:12.

Moroni 6:4.

4. The three primary purposes of the Book of Mormon are described on the title page:
   a) to show _____;
   b) so they may know _____;
   c) to convince _____.

5. Moroni 10:3 speaks of one of the purposes. We are counseled to _____
   _____. What are the benefits of this action in your life? Refer to 1
   Nephi 11:1; Helaman 10:2–5; 3 Nephi 17:2–3; Doctrine and Covenants 138:1, 11.

6. Alma 32:41 notes the three things required to nourish the word so that it can grow
   and you can partake of the fruit. List the three things.

The Prophet Joseph Smith explained why the Book of Mormon is of such value to
Latter-day Saints: "I told the brethren that the Book of Mormon was the most correct
of any book on earth, and the keystone of our religion, and a man would get nearer
to God by abiding by its precepts, than by any other book." ("Introduction," Book of
Mormon.) It helps you to draw nearer to God. Is there not something deep in your
heart that longs to draw nearer to God? If so, the Book of Mormon will help you do
so more than any other book.

It is not just that the Book of Mormon teaches you truth, though it indeed does
that. It is not just that the Book of Mormon bears testimony of Christ, though it indeed
does that too. There is something more. There is a power in the book that will begin

to flow into your life the moment you begin a serious study of the book. You will find greater power to resist temptation. You will find the power to avoid deception. You will find the power to stay on the strait and narrow path.

The scriptures are called "the words of life" (D&C 84:85), and that is especially true of the Book of Mormon. When you begin to hunger and thirst after those words, you will find life become richer in greater and greater abundance. The promises of increased love and harmony in the home, greater respect between parent and child, increased spirituality and righteousness are not idle promises—they are exactly what the Prophet Joseph Smith meant when he said the Book of Mormon will help you draw nearer to God. (See *Teachings of Ezra Taft Benson,* p. 54.)

The Book of Mormon is full of scriptures on missionary work. Elder Michael Alan De Groot sought out missionary scriptures from the Book of Mormon during and after his mission. Below is a listing by topic. Please read and ponder them. They will give you insight and understanding into the work.

The call of preaching: Enos 1:26; Alma 5:43–44, 49; 8:24; 13:6; 28:13; 39:16; 42:31; 3 Nephi 5:13; 13:25; Moroni 7:2; 8:2.

Why preach (motives): 2 Nephi 2:30; 6:3; Jacob 1:19; Mosiah 28:3; Alma 26:26, 29–30; 36:24–26.

Enthusiasm and urgency in preaching: 1 Nephi 15:25; 2 Nephi 2:8; Jacob 5:70–71; Alma 16:16–17; 29:1–3; 43:1; Helaman 15:6; Mormon 3:22.

Prayer's part: Mosiah 18:12; Alma 8:10; 31:35; Moroni 8:28.

To whom is the gospel preached? 2 Nephi 26:25–33; Alma 6:5–6; 16:14; 26:37; 37:13–15; Helaman 3:26–28; 3 Nephi 9:14; 18:25, 32.

What to preach: 1 Nephi 6:4–5; 2 Nephi 25:26; Jacob 1:7–8; 3:2; Mosiah 18:20; Alma 5:33–34; 11:22; 21:23; 37:32–34, 47; Helaman 5:11; 8:3; 3 Nephi 11:32–34, 37–41; 27:20; 28:18.

How to preach as instruments of God: Jacob 5:72; Mosiah 27:35–37; Alma 17:9, 11, 29; 21:16–17; 26:3, 22; 32:37; Ether 12:14–15.

How to preach with power and authority: 2 Nephi 25:28; 33:1; Alma 4:19; 8:32; 17:2–3; 18:34–35; 31:5; 43:2; 53:10; 62:45; Helaman 5:17–19, 49–50; 6:4–5; 7:29; 3 Nephi 6:20; 7:15–18; 11:3–5; Ether 12:2–3; Moroni 8:16, 21.

Preaching and a good example: Alma 17:25; 26:11–12; 37:6–7; 38:10–15; Helaman 7:11.

Preaching and a bad example: 2 Nephi 21:12; Alma 4:10; 39:4, 11; Helaman 4:23.

The promised destiny of preaching: Mosiah 3:20; 15:28; 27:13; 3 Nephi 5:23–26; 16:11; 20:13.

The blessings of preaching for the missionary and the convert: Jacob 5:75; Mosiah 12:21; 15:17; 26:20–21, 30; Alma 19:14, 36; 26:5–7; 48:19–20; Helaman 6:36; 10:4–5; 3 Nephi 1:23; 12:2.

THINGS TO DO

1. Read the Book of Mormon daily. Make a list of scriptures that are meaningful to you, and apply the passages to your life.

2. Start looking for scriptures in the Book of Mormon that will help your investigators make the mighty change, particularly ones that will help them keep their commitments and overcome their sins.

3. Read the following statements by President Ezra Taft Benson. Then underline or highlight important points.

You know of my great love for the Book of Mormon. Sister Benson and I try to read it every morning, and we have a great love for that book. The Book of Mormon is the instrument that God has designed to "sweep the earth as with a flood, to gather out His elect unto the New Jerusalem." This sacred volume of scripture has not been, nor is it yet, central in our preaching, our teaching, and our missionary work.
  —*Teachings of Ezra Taft Benson,* p. 60.

Just as a man does not really desire food until he is hungry, so he does not desire the salvation of Christ until he knows why he needs Christ. No one adequately and properly knows why he needs Christ until he understands and accepts the doctrine of the Fall and its effect upon all mankind. And no other book in the world explains this vital doctrine nearly as well as the Book of Mormon.
  —*Teachings of Ezra Taft Benson,* p. 28.

How important is the Book of Mormon? . . . "Take away the Book of Mormon and the revelations," [Joseph Smith] said, "and where is our religion? We have none." (*History of the Church,* 2:52.) "This generation," said the Lord to Joseph Smith, the translator, "shall have my word through you." (D&C 5:10.) And so it has. . . .

What is the major purpose of the Book of Mormon? To bring men to Christ and to be reconciled to him, and then to join his Church—in that order. (See 2 Nephi 25:23: D&C 20:11–14, 35–37.) The title page of the Book of Mormon states the book is for "the convincing of the Jew and Gentile that Jesus is the Christ, the Eternal God." The Lord further instructed that the Book of Mormon proves that "God does inspire men and call them to his holy work in this age and generation, as in generations of old." (D&C 20:11.)
  —"A New Witness for Christ," *Ensign,* November 1984, p. 6.

The honest seeker after truth can gain the testimony that Jesus is the Christ as he prayerfully ponders the inspired words of the Book of Mormon. Over one-half of all the verses in the Book of Mormon refer to our Lord. Some form of Christ's name is mentioned more frequently per verse in the Book of Mormon than even in the New Testament. He is given over one hundred different names in the Book of Mormon. Those names have a particular significance in describing His divine nature.
  —"Come unto Christ," *Ensign,* November 1987, p. 83.

Here, then, is a procedure to handle most objections through the use of the Book of Mormon. First, understand the objection. Second, give the answer from revelation. Third, show how the correctness of the answer really depends on whether or not we have modern revelation through modern prophets. Fourth, explain that whether or not we have modern prophets and revelation really depends on whether the Book of Mormon is true. Therefore, the only problem the objector has to resolve for himself is whether the Book of Mormon is true. For if the Book of Mormon is true, then Jesus is the Christ, Joseph Smith was His prophet, The Church of Jesus Christ of Latter-day Saints is true, and it is being led today by a prophet receiving revelation.
  —*Teachings of Ezra Taft Benson,* pp. 61–62.

The Book of Mormon brings men to Christ through two basic means. First, it tells in a plain manner of Christ and His gospel. It testifies of His divinity and of the necessity for a Redeemer and the need of our putting trust in Him. It bears witness of the Fall and the Atonement and the first principles of the gospel, including our need of a broken heart and a contrite spirit and a spiritual rebirth. It proclaims we must endure to the end in righteousness and live the moral life of a Saint. Second, the Book of Mormon exposes the enemies of Christ. It confounds false doctrines and lays down contention. (See 1 Nephi 3:12.) It fortifies the humble followers of Christ against the evil designs, strategies, and doctrines of the devil in our day. The type of apostates in the Book of Mormon are similar to the type we have today. God, with His infinite foreknowledge, so molded the Book of Mormon that we might see the error and know how to combat false educational, political, religious, and philosophical concepts of our time.

—*Teachings of Ezra Taft Benson,* p. 56.

The Book of Mormon must be reenthroned in the minds and hearts of our people. We must honor it by reading it, by studying it, by taking its precepts into our lives and transforming them into lives required of the true followers of Christ. . . . President Joseph Fielding Smith said: "It seems to me that any member of this Church would never be satisfied until he or she had read the Book of Mormon time and time again, and thoroughly considered it so that he or she could bear witness that it is in very deed a record with the inspiration of the Almighty upon it, and that its history is true. . . . No member of this Church can stand approved in the presence of God who has not seriously and carefully read the Book of Mormon." (In Conference Report, October 1961, p. 18.)

—"The Gift of Modern Revelation," *Ensign,* November 1986, p. 80.

I have a conviction: The more we teach and preach from the Book of Mormon, the more we shall please the Lord and the greater will be our power of speaking. By so doing, we shall greatly increase our converts, both within the Church and among those we proselyte. The Lord expects us to use this book, and we remain under His condemnation if we do not (see D&C 84:57). Our commission then is to teach the principles of the gospel which are in the Bible and the Book of Mormon. "These shall be their teachings, as they shall be directed by the Spirit." (D&C 42:13.) . . .

We must make the Book of Mormon a center focus of study because it was written for our day. The Nephites never had the book, neither did the Lamanites of ancient times. It was meant for us. Mormon wrote near the end of the Nephite civilization. Under the inspiration of God, who sees all things from the beginning, he abridged centuries of records, choosing the stories, speeches, and events that would be most helpful to us.

—*Teachings of Ezra Taft Benson,* p. 58.

We have not been using the Book of Mormon as we should. Our homes are not as strong unless we are using it to bring our children to Christ. Our families may be corrupted by worldly trends and teachings unless we know how to use the book to expose and combat the falsehoods in socialism, organic evolution, rationalism, humanism, and so forth. Our missionaries are not as effective unless they are "hissing forth" with it. Social, ethical, cultural, or educational converts will not survive under the heat of the day unless their taproots go down to the fulness of the gospel which the Book of Mormon contains. Our Church classes are not as spirit-filled unless we hold it up as a standard. And our nation will continue to degenerate unless we read and heed the words of the God of this land, Jesus Christ, and quit building up and upholding the secret combinations which the Book of Mormon tells us proved the downfall of both previous American civilizations.

—*A Witness and a Warning*, p. 6.

The Book of Mormon must be the heart of our missionary work in every mission of the Church if we are to come out from under this condemnation (see D&C 84:56–57). And what a marvelous missionary tool it is! Already we see an increase in baptisms, which testifies to the power of this sacred volume.

—*Teachings of Ezra Taft Benson*, p. 203.

Take time daily to read the scriptures together as a family. Individual scripture reading is important, but family scripture reading is vital. Reading the Book of Mormon together as a family will especially bring increased spirituality into your home and will give both parents and children the power to resist temptation and to have the Holy Ghost as their constant companion. I promise you that the Book of Mormon will change the lives of your family.

—*Teachings of Ezra Taft Benson*, p. 517.

Once we realize how the Lord feels about this book it should not surprise us that He also gives us solemn warnings about how we receive it. After indicating that those who receive the Book of Mormon with faith, working righteousness, will receive a crown of eternal glory (see D&C 20:14), the Lord follows with this warning: "But those who harden their hearts in unbelief, and reject it, it shall turn to their own condemnation" (D&C 20:15).

—*Teachings of Ezra Taft Benson*, p. 52.

DILIGENCE WITH FAITH
IN THE STRENGTH OF THE LORD

President Benson has said, "I have often said one of the greatest secrets of missionary work is work! If a missionary works, he will get the Spirit; if he gets the Spirit, he will teach by the Spirit; and if he teaches by the Spirit, he will touch the hearts of the people and he will be happy. There will be no homesickness, no worrying about families, for all time and talents and interests are centered on the work of the ministry. Work, work, work—there is no satisfactory substitute, especially in missionary work." (*Teachings of Ezra Taft Benson,* p. 200.)

1. What kind of work ethic is described in Doctrine and Covenants 4:2?

2. How did the Lord describe Nephi's work in Helaman 10:4–5?

3. What did Mormon teach his son, Moroni, in regard to how he should labor, and why? Moroni 9:6.

4. In Alma 32:42–43, the Lord explains the principle of nourishing the word and describes the rewards. What is required to nourish the word, and what is the result?

5. The pointers on the Liahona worked according to "_____ which [the Nephites gave] unto them." 1 Nephi 16:28.

6. Many blessings are noted in the following scriptures concerning diligence. Describe each.

   Mosiah 7:33.

   Alma 12:9.

   Alma 49:30.

   Moroni 8:26.

   Doctrine and Covenants 18:8.

   Doctrine and Covenants 59:4

   Doctrine and Covenants 107:99–100.

   Doctrine and Covenants 130:19.

7. How did Nephi and Lehi work the mighty change among the people? Ether 12:14.

8. Through _____, you can do all things the Lord knows are expedient for him. Moroni 7:33; 10:23.

9. How do you show your faith? James 2:18.

10. Why are men given weaknesses? Ether 12:27.

11. How can you grow in humility and faith? Helaman 3:35.

12. How did Nephi build the ship? 1 Nephi 17:49–51.

13. Why did Nephi and Lehi (the sons of Helaman) and the sons of Mosiah enjoy such great missionary success? Ether 12:14–15.

14. How do you get the "strength of the Lord"? Moses 1:20.

President Benson has stressed the ethic of work, work, work. Those who are attentive to their preparation, who take great care to do every needful thing in a spirit of constant concern for the work, who are conscientious about studying the scriptures daily, who work hard in every sense of the word, who persevere in the quest to qualify for their mission will be tireless, diligent missionaries. They will be blessed! As you exercise your faith, you will be a mighty instrument in the Lord's hands. Remember, faith has power to do all things in righteousness.

The Lord will use the weak and the simple to thrash the nations. Ammon said it best: "Yea, I know that I am nothing; as to my strength I am weak; therefore I will not boast of myself, but I will boast of my God, for in his strength I can do all things; yea, behold, many mighty miracles we have wrought in this land, for which we will praise his name forever." (Alma 26:12.) When you become totally dependent on God, the outcome of your endeavors is no longer determined by the world. This dependence is an act of humility. Spiritual growth is directly proportional to your humility and dependence on the Lord. As you become strong in humility and firm in your faith, you gain strength in the Lord.

THINGS TO DO

1. Go out with the missionaries for an entire day.
2. Do the best job (with every fiber of your being) in a given task that you can do— i.e., clean your room, clean the yard, work at the chapel or on a welfare assignment.
3. Let your homework from school be a test of how diligently you can work and do your best.

4. Think, ponder, and meditate about the work. Remember, faith is exercised in part by mental exertion and is strengthened by the Holy Ghost.

5. Read the following statements by the prophets. Then underline or highlight important points.

Ezra Taft Benson: You must not allow yourselves to become discouraged. Missionary work brings joy, optimism, and happiness. Don't give Satan an opportunity to discourage you. Here again, work is the answer. The Lord has given us a key by which we can overcome discouragement: "Come unto me, all ye that labour and are heavy laden, and I will give you rest. Take my yoke upon you, and learn of me; for I am meek and lowly in heart; and ye shall find rest unto your souls. For my yoke is easy and my burden is light." (Matthew 11:28–30.)
  —*Teachings of Ezra Taft Benson,* pp. 205–6.

Ezra Taft Benson: The busy missionary is the happy missionary. I cannot recall a missionary who was really active and busy ever going astray. Occasionally we have missionaries who make mistakes. It usually starts when they become idle, when they stay in their lodgings when they ought to be out with the people, when they try to find excuses for not going out and tracting and knocking on doors and holding meetings with the people. Occasionally you will find a missionary who is looking for excuses for not going out—who can look out the window and see a storm coming when there isn't any, who can see rain when it isn't raining. The important thing is to get out with the people, to keep active, to be devoted. Do not sleep longer than is needful. The same Lord who gave the Word of Wisdom in the 89th section also gave that instruction in the 88th section, and it is just as binding as the counsel that you are not to use tobacco or alcoholic beverages. So cease from all lightmindedness, cease to sleep longer than is needful, and retire to your bed early. [See D&C 88:121, 124.] You will be more effective, you will do more work, you will be happier, and you will have better health.
  —*God, Family, Country,* p. 60.

Orson Pratt: I will prophesy that the power of the Lord God of Israel will be with you to a far greater extent than it has been poured out in days that are passed; and the way will be open before you, and the Lord will visit the hearts of the people before you arrive among them, and make manifest to them by visions and dreams that you are the servants of God, before they shall see your faces. And you will receive heavenly visions to comfort you, and dreams to give you knowledge of the things of God, if you prove faithful before him. I will prophesy this in the name of the Lord God of Israel; and you will find that his power will be more conspicuously made manifest through your administrations on these missions than has ever taken place since the rise of this Church.
  —*Masterful Discourses and Writings of Orson Pratt,* compiled N. B. Lundwall (Salt Lake City: Bookcraft, 1962), p. 35.

Brigham Young: I would like to impress upon the minds of the brethren, that he who goes forth in the name of the Lord, trusting in Him with all his heart, will never want for wisdom to answer any question that is asked him, or to give any counsel that may be required to lead the people in the way of life and salvation, and he will never be confounded worlds without end. . . . Go in the name of the Lord, trust in the name of the Lord, lean upon the Lord, and call upon the Lord fervently and without ceasing, and pay no attention to the world.

—*Journal of Discourses,* 12:34.

Spencer W. Kimball: Brothers and sisters—all fellow members in this most important work—we must not slacken our hands in this work. Not only is our eternal welfare at stake, but also the eternal welfare of many of our brothers and sisters who are not now members of this church.

—"It Becometh Every Man," *Ensign,* October 1977, p. 7.

Spencer W. Kimball: Immerse yourself in your work, totally, and forget clocks. It is on the second mile where the honest in heart are often found.

—*The Teachings of Spencer W. Kimball,* p. 582.

THE WORK

FINDING

TEACHING

THE DISCUSSIONS

BRINGING SOULS TO CHRIST

IN THE FIELD

JOY OF THE WORK

CHAPTER 16

FINDING

Finding is the beginning of the teaching and converting process. You have to have *someone* to share the gospel with. As a disciple of the Lord, your duty is to share the gospel by opening your mouth and in living your life in such a way that people will desire to hear the word of the Lord.

1. Why are many people kept from the truth? Doctrine and Covenants 123:12. What can you do about this situation?

2. As a baptized member of the Church, what is one of your duties pertaining to missionary work as described in Mosiah 18:9?

3. The Lord told you in Doctrine and Covenants 88:81 to _____ _____ .

4. What happens if you don't open your mouth? Doctrine and Covenants 60:2–3.

5. What happens if you do open your mouth?
   Doctrine and Covenants 33:8–11.

Doctrine and Covenants 84:85, 87–88.

Doctrine and Covenants 100:5–8.

6. Where should you open your mouth? Doctrine and Covenants 24:12.

As a member of the Church, you can assist the work greatly by finding people for the missionaries to teach. As a missionary in the field, you eventually learn how to interact with others in such a way that you will be comfortable in "opening your mouth." You will start gospel conversations. You will be inspired to say the right thing at the right time in the right way, and you will become a mighty instrument in the Lord's hands.

As you gain courage through obedience, faith, knowledge, love, and preparation, you can overcome fear. Testimony after testimony from the missionaries says, "Just do it. The Lord will help you." The joy of assisting in the work is wonderful. (See Alma 36:24; D&C 18:10–16). Remember, the Lord will assist you in finding those who will receive his message. (See 1 Nephi 3:7; Alma 26:12; Moroni 7:33.)

THINGS TO DO

1. Start a gospel conversation with a nonmember acquaintance in a store, on the street, in a shop, on a bus, or on the plane—wherever and whenever you can.

2. Pray for the missionaries to be successful in finding those who will come unto Christ.

3. Read the following statements by the prophets. Then underline or highlight important points.

Ezra Taft Benson: The Book of Mormon is the great standard we are to use in our missionary work. It shows that Joseph Smith was a prophet. It contains the words of Christ, and its great mission is to bring men to Christ. All other things are secondary. The golden question of the Book of Mormon is "Do you want to learn more of Christ?" The Book of Mormon is the great finder of the golden contact. It does not contain things which are "pleasing unto the world," and so the worldly are not interested in it. It is a great sieve. (See 1 Nephi 6:5.)
   —*Teachings of Ezra Taft Benson,* p. 203.

Spencer W. Kimball: I repeat my witness that [the Lord] will unlock doors and His promises may be relied upon. I know He will stay the opposition. He will mellow hearts and He will pave the way if we have faith to pursue.
   —*Teachings of Spencer W. Kimball,* p. 57.

Spencer W. Kimball: We are still just scratching the surface of the needs of our Father's other children who dwell upon the earth. Many still hunger and thirst after truth and are kept from it only "because they know not where to find it." (Doctrine and Covenants 123:12.) There are still more places to go than there are full-time missionaries and organized missions to serve them. There are still millions more being born, living, and dying, than are hearing testimonies borne to them by the servants of the Lord.

All of this means, quite frankly, brethren, that we cannot share the gospel with every nation, kindred, tongue, and people with [the present number of] missionaries (as wonderful as they are), but we must have several million more to help them. We must, therefore, involve the members of the Church more effectively in missionary work. Member-missionary work is the key to the future growth of the Church, and it is one of the great keys to the individual growth of our members.

—Regional Representatives' Seminar, 3 October 1980.

CHAPTER 17

TEACHING

You are commanded to teach the gospel truths by the power of the Spirit. When people feel the Spirit, you help them recognize it and act upon those feelings by inviting them to make commitments. Keeping these commitments assists them in the conversion process, that they might partake of the goodness of God. Then through faith unto repentance, they are baptized and receive the Holy Ghost.

1. What do you teach? Doctrine and Covenants 42:12.

2. How do you teach? Doctrine and Covenants 42:13–14.

3. Teaching and the process of conversion can be done only by the Spirit. Doctrine and Covenants 50:13–14, 17–22 describe this process.

    a) Unto what were you ordained? Doctrine and Covenants 50:13–14.

    b) How do you preach the word? Doctrine and Covenants 50:17.

    c) How do people receive the word? Doctrine and Covenants 50:19.

d) What causes both the teacher and the learner to rejoice? Doctrine and Covenants 50:21–22.

4. Describe the truths concerning the missionary depicted in Doctrine and Covenants 50:26–30.

5. We must remember the relative importance of the teacher and the learner. Describe the relationship. Alma 1:26.

6. Who carries the word to the hearts of the learner? 2 Nephi 33:1.

7. Alma, at the ends of chapters 37, 38, and 42 of Alma, cautions his sons to preach the word and be sober. To be sober in these cases is to be serious and solemn-minded because of the sacredness of the duty. In which verses in chapters 37, 38, and 42 is this mentioned?

8. How do you teach with the power and authority of God? Alma 17:2–3.

9. How should we preach the word? Doctrine and Covenants 38:41.

10. Alma gave excellent advice to his son Helaman. Fill in the blanks. Alma 37:33–37:
"Preach unto them _____, and _____ on the Lord Jesus Christ; teach them
to _____ themselves and to be _____ and _____ in heart; teach them to
_____ of the devil, with their _____ on the Lord Jesus Christ.
Teach them to never be _____ works, but to be _____
and _____ in heart; for such shall _____ to their souls. O, remember,
my son, and learn _____ in thy _____; yea, learn in thy youth to keep the
commandments of God. Yea, and _____ unto God for _____; yea,
let _____ be unto the Lord, and withersoever thou goest let it be in
the Lord; yea, let _____ be directed unto the Lord; yea, let the
_____ of thy heart be placed _____ forever. _____ with
the Lord in all thy doings, and he will _____ thee for good; yea, when thou
_____ at night _____ unto the Lord, that he may _____ you in your sleep;
and when thou risest in the morning let thy _____ be full of _____ unto
God; and if you do these things, ye shall be _____ at the last day."

11. Alma also counseled his son Shiblon. Fill in the blanks. Alma 38:9–14:
"And now, my son, I have told you this that ye may _____, that
ye may learn of me that there is _____ or means whereby man
_____, only in and through _____. Behold, he is the _____ and the
_____ of the world. Behold, he is the _____ and _____. And
now, as ye have begun to _____ even so I would that ye should
_____; and I would that ye would be _____ and _____ in
all things. See that ye are _____ unto _____; yea, see that ye
_____ in your own wisdom, nor of your much strength. Use
_____, but _____; and also see that ye _____,
that ye may be _____; see that ye _____. Do not
pray as the Zoramites do, for ye have seen that they _____,
and to be _____. Do not say: O God, I thank thee that we
are better than our brethren; but _____: O Lord, _____,
and _____ —yea, _____ your _____ before God
_____."

When teaching, using the Book of Mormon to help the investigator is important.
As you root them to the book, you will root them to Christ. This is crucial. You help
bring people to Christ, not to you and your sociality. Stephen Graham has developed
this process of using the Book of Mormon in teaching:

1. Do they (the investigators) know I really care?

2. Do I know how they feel and think concerning themselves as these relate to the
   discussion? For instance, does the investigator feel as if he can't keep the Word of
   Wisdom?

3. What in the Book of Mormon could I use to help the investigator?

1 Nephi 3:7	The Lord will prepare a way.
Moroni 7:33	Through faith I can do what the Lord wants.
Ether 12:27	I'm given weaknesses to humble me so I will depend on the Lord.
Alma 26:12	In the strength of the Lord, I can do all things.

4. As investigators feel the fruits of the Spirit (see D&C 11:12–13, Galatians 5:22), they will have a desire to do good. I need to make them aware of the Spirit.

5. Invite them to live the Word of Wisdom.

Teaching by the Spirit is the key. As you are humble, meek, mild, bold in faith but not overbearing, teaching investigators clearly so they understand, using personal experiences, you will become a true ambassador of Christ. You will teach with power and authority to the convincing them of the truth—and you will have joy.

THINGS TO DO

1. Practice giving Discussions 1 and 2. Perhaps read them to a member of your family or to a friend.

2. Go with the full-time missionaries to teach a discussion.

3. Make a list of scriptures that can help your investigator make and keep commitments.

4. Read the following statements by the prophets. Then underline or highlight important points.

Brigham Young: If those who are going to preach do not go with that faith that pertains to eternal life, and that spirit that is like a well of water, springing up into everlasting life, their labours will be vain. They may be the best theoretical theologians in the world—may be able to preach a Bible and a half in a sermon, to read history without a book, and understand all the dealings with men from the days of Adam till now; and, without the Spirit of the living God to guide them, they will not be able to accomplish anything to their credit towards building up his kingdom. They must realize that success in preaching the Gospel springs not from the wisdom of this world. They must so live as to enjoy the power of God.
—*Journal of Discourses,* 8:70–71.

Brigham Young: Let one go forth who is careful to logically prove all he says by numerous quotations from the revelations, and let another travel with him who can say, by the power of the Holy Ghost, Thus saith the Lord, and tell what the people should believe—what they should do—how they should live, and teach them to yield to the principles of salvation,—though he may not be capable of producing a single logical argument—though he may tremble under a sense of his weakness, cleaving to the Lord for strength, as such men generally do, you will invariably find that the man who testifies by the power of the Holy Ghost will convince and gather many more of the honest and upright than will the merely logical reasoner.
—*Journal of Discourses,* 8:53.

Joseph Smith: Remember that your business is to preach the Gospel in all humility and meekness, and warn sinners to repent and come to Christ.

Avoid contentions and vain disputes with men of corrupt minds, who do not desire to know the truth. Remember that "it is a day of warning, and not a day of many words." If they receive not your testimony in one place, flee to another, remembering to cast no reflections, nor throw out any bitter sayings. If you do your duty, it will be just as well with you, as though all men embraced the Gospel.

—*Teachings of the Prophet Joseph Smith,* p. 43.

Joseph Smith: The Elders would go forth, and each must stand for himself . . . to go in all meekness, in sobriety, and preach Jesus Christ and Him crucified; not to contend with others on account of their faith, or systems of religion, but pursue a steady course. This I delivered by way of commandment; and all who observe it not, will pull down persecution upon their heads, while those who do, shall always be filled with the Holy Ghost; this I pronounced as a prophecy, and sealed with hosanna and amen.

—*History of the Church,* 2:431.

Wilford Woodruff: The whole secret of our success as far as making converts is concerned is, that we preach the same Gospel in all its simplicity and plainness that Jesus preached, and that the Holy Ghost rests upon those who receive it, filling their hearts with joy and gladness unspeakable, and making them as one; and they then know of the doctrine for themselves whether it be of God or man.

—*Journal of Discourses,* 23:129.

THE DISCUSSIONS

The discussions are designed to help people understand and appreciate the doctrines and principles of the gospel of Jesus Christ. The commitment pattern (a methodology of expressing love) is used in *finding, teaching, baptizing, fellowshipping, and working with others.* As people feel the Spirit during the discussions, invite them to make commitments, and then follow through to help them keep those commitments, thus bringing about the conversion process in their lives.

Following are the principles in each discussion. With the help of the scriptures, your discussions, and the *Missionary Gospel Study Guide,* make a statement or write out a scripture that teaches that principle.

Discussion 1: The Plan of Our Heavenly Father
Principles

1. The plan of our Heavenly Father

2. The divine sonship of Jesus Christ

3. How the plan has been revealed

4. The Prophet Joseph Smith: a modern witness of Jesus Christ

5. The Book of Mormon: Another Testament of Jesus Christ

6. The Holy Ghost: a witness of the truth

Discussion 2: The Gospel of Jesus Christ
Principles
1. Salvation from physical death

2. Salvation from sin

3. Faith in Christ

4. Repentance

5. Baptism by immersion for the remission of sins

6. The gift of the Holy Ghost

7. Obedience to the commandments of God

Discussion 3: The Restoration
Principles
1. Truth versus error

2. Apostasy

3. The restoration of truth

4. The restoration of the Church

5. Membership in the true church

6. Attending church meetings and partaking of the sacrament

Discussion 4: Eternal Progression
Principles
1. Our premortal existence

2. Mortal life on earth

3. Life after death

4. Work for the dead

5. The eternal family

6. Chastity

7. The Word of Wisdom

Discussion 5: Living a Christlike Life
Principles

1. The two great commandments

2. Sacrifice brings blessings

3. Fasting and fast offerings

4. Tithing

Discussion 6: Membership in the Kingdom
Principles

1. The role of Jesus Christ in the plan of salvation

2. Exaltation through Christ and his church

3. The mission of the Church: perfecting the Saints

4. The mission of the Church: proclaiming the gospel

5. The mission of the Church: redeeming the dead

6. The strait and narrow path

As you come to understand and appreciate the doctrines taught in the six discussions, you will realize the beauty, the truth, and the importance of teaching our Heavenly

Father's children the word of God. As you teach by the Spirit, the words will be carried to their hearts. Teach in a pleasant atmosphere with love that they might taste of the gospel of Jesus Christ through the blessings of the Spirit. Having felt and recognized the Spirit, investigators should accept the invitation to commit to be baptized.

THINGS TO DO

1. Using the *Missionary Gospel Study Plan,* make a plan with completion dates to understand the principles and doctrines taught in each discussion.

2. Read and study the introduction to the discussions.

3. Read through and practice each discussion with a friend.

CHAPTER 19

BRINGING SOULS TO CHRIST

The *Missionary Guide* is the wonderful tool the Lord has given us to train missionaries. The scriptures are full of examples of great missionaries and teachers who have brought people to Christ by teaching them his Gospel in the spirit of truth. (See Mosiah 2–6; Alma 17–26.) King Benjamin and Ammon gained the respect and love of those whom they taught the gospel. They helped them feel the Spirit. They invited them to come unto Christ. They continued with them to strengthen them in the gospel.

1. It is important to understand the commitments and covenants one makes at baptism. List those again from Doctrine and Covenants 20:37 and Mosiah 18:8–10.

2. What do you promise to do as you renew your covenants through the sacrament? Doctrine and Covenants 20:77, 79; or Moroni 4:3 and 5:2.

3. What do fellow church members do after a person has joined the Church? Moroni 6:4.

4. What do you do to help your convert understand the importance of family history and temple work? Doctrine and Covenants 128:15, 24.

Those whom you assist in coming into the Church should alway be in your prayers. Do those things that make them feel welcome and loved. The sociality of the Church would suggest that we are friends as well as brothers and sisters and that we have love and concern for all mankind continuously.

THINGS TO DO

1. Study all the principles of the commitment pattern in the *Missionary Guide.*

2. Study the principles of baptism and fellowshipping in the *Missionary Guide.*

3. Read the following statements by the prophets. Then underline or highlight the important points.

Spencer W. Kimball: Actually, the missionary does not convert anyone: the Holy Ghost does the converting. The power of conversion is directly associated with the Holy Ghost, for no person can be truly converted and know that Jesus is the Christ save by the power of the Holy Ghost.

—*Teachings of Spencer W. Kimball,* p. 570.

Henry D. Moyle: Some may ask the question as to how we convert others to the truth. The answer is, we do not. Conversion comes from above. Our part in this work is to plant the seeds of truth. These seeds are born of our conviction when we testify of the divine mission of Jesus Christ, the Son of the Living God, who offered himself as a sacrifice for the sins of the world. We rely upon the gift and power of the Holy Ghost to carry our message in the hearts of our listeners and witness unto them the truthfulness of our stated conviction.

—Conference Report, April 1961, pp. 101–2.

Spencer W. Kimball: As a vital link in the conversion process, we should bear our testimonies that the gospel is true; our testimonies may well be the spark that ignites the conversion process. Consequently, we have a double responsibility: we must testify of the things we know, feel, and have felt, and we must live so the Holy Ghost can be with us and convey our words in power to the heart of the investigator.

—*Teachings of Spencer W. Kimball,* p. 138.

Ezra Taft Benson: We desire all potential members to be friendshipped. Our youth should be involved in missionary work. Some of our finest converts come through the young people of the Church. We hope that home teachers are working closely with part-member families to see that the gospel is taught to the nonmembers in that household.

—*Teachings of Ezra Taft Benson,* p. 209.

Harold B. Lee: We must extend the hand of fellowship to men everywhere, and to all who are truly converted and who wish to join the Church and partake of the many rewarding opportunities to be found therein. . . . We ask the Church members to strive to emulate the example of our Lord and Master Jesus Christ, who gave us the new commandment that we should love one another.

—Quoted by Spencer W. Kimball, in *Faith Precedes the Miracle* (Salt Lake City: Deseret Book Co., 1972), p. 296.

Neal A. Maxwell: The Church is for the perfecting of the Saints, hence new arrivals are entitled to expect instant community but not instant sainthood—either in themselves or in others. It takes time and truth working patiently together to produce the latter in all of us.

—Conference Report, October 1980, p. 18.

Mark E. Petersen: Instruction in the gospel without fellowship in the Church is as incomplete as baptism without confirmation.

—Conference Report, April 1961, p. 90.

Joseph Smith: Nothing is so much calculated to lead people to forsake sin as to take them by the hand, and watch over them with tenderness.

—*History of the Church,* 5:23–24.

CHAPTER 20

IN THE FIELD

Learning to prepare for the mission field can reduce your anxiety and help you prepare to overcome the trials and tribulations that will arise. There is opposition. People are human—they are not always at their best, and this includes members as well as missionaries. Plan today to prepare well—so that when you go into the field, you can begin to work immediately. Plan to return with honor, having no regrets, by working hard and being obedient.

1. If ye are not _____ ye are not mine. Doctrine and Covenants 38:27. What is the significance of this in regard to your companionship and the work?

2. During tribulation, what great attribute do you need to exercise? _____. Doctrine and Covenants 54:10.

3. You also need these attributes to nurture the word in your life. _____ _____. Alma 32:41–43.

4. Enduring tribulation well brings much to your life. What are some of the rewards? Doctrine and Covenants 58:2–3.

Doctrine and Covenants 103:12–13.

Doctrine and Covenants 122:5–8.

Doctrine and Covenants 138:12–19.

5. Question 4 brings to mind the great experiences of growth that come through trials and tribulations. What kind of attitude would we develop in order to cope with tribulation? 1 Peter 4:12–16.

6. Afflictions are often for our good. Many principles resulting from or accompanying affliction are taught in the following scriptures. Describe them.
   2 Nephi 2:2.

   Alma 34:40–41.

   Alma 62:41.

   Helaman 12:3.

   Doctrine and Covenants 24:1.

   Doctrine and Covenants 93:42.

   Doctrine and Covenants 98:3.

When you suffer for the Lord, you are blessed. Afflictions and trials can be used for your growth as you turn to the Lord in faith and prayer. Remember, as a full-time missionary in the field, you represent the Lord Jesus Christ as a minister. You minister to the people by preaching the word and doing acts of kindness. Study the things in the *Missionary Guide* that make for good companionships. The Lord will bless you. He will be in your midst. You will be in the world but not of the world. Pray with all the energy of your heart to be even as he is.

THINGS TO DO

1. Go on a mini-mission for a few weeks with the full-time missionaries.

2. Visit with returned missionaries and get the feeling of the work.

3. Make a list of the afflictions that you have overcome in the strength of the Lord.

4. Read the chapter on companions in the *Missionary Guide*.

5. Read the following statements by the prophets. Then underline or highlight important points.

Brigham Young: If you go on a mission to preach the Gospel with lightness and frivolity in your hearts, looking for this and that, and to learn what is in the world, and not having your minds riveted—yes, I may say riveted—on the cross of Christ, you will go and return in vain. Go forth weeping, bearing precious seed, full of the power of God, and full of faith.
—*Discourses of Brigham Young,* p. 325.

Brigham Young: Come home with your heads up. Keep yourselves clean, from the crowns of your heads to the soles of your feet; be pure in heart,—otherwise you will return bowed down in spirit and with a fallen countenance, and will feel as though you never could rise again.
—*Discourses of Brigham Young,* p. 328.

Spencer W. Kimball: Getting along with missionary companions teaches unselfishness. I find some difficulty between missionaries. Brothers and sisters, that's one of the tests for which you are here on the proving ground. If you can't get along with your companion, how can you get along with the person you choose to live with for the rest of your life? For your own sake, you must fit into your companion's life and adjust. Perhaps your homes are different. Grit your teeth and say, "I am going to give 90 percent and I will only take 10 percent." . . . You must think of the other, love him more than your own self, and then you will have success. Marriage is not something which when you press a button you get happiness. You have to make happiness in marriage the same as in the mission field. . . . Instead of fighting for your own pleasure, you are fighting for the pleasure of the other. . . .

Missionaries are responsible for companions. Now I ask, nearly every time I interview a missionary, "Suppose you and your companion are in a distant town and he begins to flirt and break all the mission rules, where is your loyalty?" He is puzzled at first. He would like to be true to a fellow missionary. I know what is in his mind. I ask him where is his loyalty, to a lawbreaker or to the kingdom; to a companion who will not yield to the proper rules and regulations, or to your God in heaven?
—*Teachings of Spencer W. Kimball,* pp. 579–80.

Ezra Taft Benson: I hope you feel you have the best companion in the world. I hope you draw close to each other as companions, that you uphold and sustain each other before the Saints, before our friends, before the world. I have seen many examples of this, but one of the most impressive occurred in Philadelphia some years ago. I had been in a meeting of agricultural leaders all day, and in the evening I left my hotel to mail a couple of letters. As I walked into the post office I heard the strains of a familiar Mormon hymn coming through the window from the opposite side. I dropped my letters in the box, walked over to the window, and looked out, and there were two young men in dark suits standing on the steps of the post office holding a street meeting. One of them was speaking and the other was holding in one hand two hats and in the other some copies of the Book of Mormon and some tracts. When they finished their meeting I went out and introduced myself. Then I said to the young man who was holding the hats and the copies of the Book of Mormon, "What were you doing while your companion was speaking?" His answer was most satisfying. He said, "Brother Benson, I was praying to the Lord that he would say the right thing that would touch the hearts of the people who were listening."

That's the kind of support I am referring to. When you reach the point where you can enjoy and rejoice in the success of your companion, even when that success exceeds your own, then you have got the real missionary spirit, the real unselfish spirit of love, the spirit of the gospel. When you can rejoice in the success of your companion, then you've got a spirit that will make you effective as a missionary. Then you will really be truly, truly happy. Then you will have lost yourself in the service of this wonderful gospel, in service to our Father's children—the greatest work in all the world.

—*God, Family, Country*, pp. 65–66.

CHAPTER 21

JOY OF THE WORK

A constant phrase echoes over the pulpit as the returning missionary speaks at his welcome home: "They were the happiest two years of my life." Being a missionary is hard work. There are difficult times. The work requires sacrifice. Why are missionaries then so grateful, and why do they feel so much joy?

1. When a missionary is truly converted, he expresses the feelings of Alma. What were Alma's feelings? Alma 29:9–10; 36:24.

2. The Lord expressed joy in having the people's faith increase. (See 3 Nephi 17:20.) What does Doctrine and Covenants 18:10–16 indicate will be your joy?

3. Alma 22:15–16 indicates what is required to be filled with joy. What is it?

4. Why were the people happy? Mosiah 2:41.

To feel happy and make your joy full, make your commitment to serve the Lord as a missionary. You can find joy and happiness as you help people come unto Christ. Pray for the missionaries. Pray for countries to open their doors. Pray for all those who are investigating the Church. Pray for all mankind, that their hearts will be softened and will open, that they might hear the word of God. The joy you experience as you help others taste of the gospel of Jesus Christ will be great. Knowing you are doing the will of your Heavenly Father will bring you even greater happiness and joy.

THINGS TO DO

1. Attend a baptism.

2. Talk to a new convert concerning his or her conversion.

3. Read in a journal or in a history of the Church about some of the early converts.

4. Read the following statements by the prophets. Then underline or highlight important points.

Ezra Taft Benson: In this work we are never alone. This is the Lord's work. These are His children we are working with. This is His great program; and He will not permit us to fail. He loves these children we are working with; they are His children—His sons and daughters. He loves them even as we love our own, even with a deeper love; and He will not permit us to fail if we will do our part. God bless us that we might measure up that we might receive joy and happiness in our service in our Father's kingdom.

—*Teachings of Ezra Taft Benson,* pp. 207–8.

Heber J. Grant: In all my labors I got nearer to the Lord, and accomplished more, and had more joy while in the mission field than ever before or since. Man is that he may have joy, and the joy that I had in the mission field was superior to any I have ever experienced elsewhere. Get it into your hearts, young people, to prepare yourselves to go out into the world where you can get on your knees and draw nearer to the Lord than in any other labor.

—"The President Speaks: Excerpts from the Utterances of Heber J. Grant," *Improvement Era,* November 1936, p. 659.

Thomas S. Monson: We [the Church] care because the Lord, who knows the source of all happiness, has asked us to do it [share the gospel with others] and has assured us blessings and happiness and joy if we will do it. We care because when we share the gospel with others, we unavoidably get outside of ourselves: we think and pray and work for the blessing of others, and this only further enriches and quickens us by the Holy Spirit. The list of by-products to ourselves is endless—growth in our testimonies, growth in our knowledge of the gospel, growth in our faith, more answered prayers. The eternal truth is: that which we willingly share, we keep; and that which we selfishly keep to ourselves, we lose. We care because we want all of our members everywhere to be happy. Is there any better reason?

—"Status Report on Missionary Work," *Ensign,* October 1977, p. 11.

George Albert Smith: It is not an easy task; it is not a pleasant thing, perhaps, to be called out into the world, to leave our dear ones, but I say to you that it will purchase for those who are faithful, for those who discharge that obligation as they may be required, peace and happiness beyond all understanding, and will prepare them that, in due time, when life's labor is complete, they will stand in the presence of their Maker, accepted of Him because of what they have done.

—Conference Report, April 1922, p. 53.

George Albert Smith: We spend most of our time, many of us, seeking the things of this life that we will be compelled to leave when we go from here, yet there are the immortal souls around us whom, if we would, we could teach and inspire to investigate the truth, and implant in their hearts a knowledge that God lives. What treasure in all

the world could be so precious to us, for we would have their gratitude here and their everlasting and eternal appreciation in the world to come.
    —Conference Report, October 1916, p. 50.

Ezra Taft Benson: I challenge you to enjoy your call and to magnify it completely. Be happy and joyful in the service of the Lord. Love missionary work with all your heart. I promise you that as you magnify your call this will be the sweetest and most glorious experience you have had in Church service to this time.
    —Teachings of Ezra Taft Benson, p. 205.

Orson F. Whitney: There is no joy that can compare with that of a missionary who has been made the instrument for the salvation of a soul.
    —Conference Report, April 1918, p. 73.

Ezra Taft Benson: You face the happiest years of your lives. I know whereof I speak. I have been there. I have tasted the joy of missionary work. There is no work in all the world that can bring an individual greater joy and happiness. I pray your joy will be full, and like Ammon of old, you will be able to say: "I do not boast in my own strength, nor in my own wisdom; but behold, my joy is full, yea, my heart is brim with joy, and I will rejoice in my God. Yea, I know that I am nothing; as to my strength I am weak; therefore I will not boast of myself, but I will boast of my God, for in his strength I can do all things; yea, behold, many mighty miracles we have wrought in this land, for which we will praise his name forever." (Alma 26:11–12.)
    —Teachings of Ezra Taft Benson, p. 213.